Praise for
Collaborate: The Art of We

"'Too many cooks spoil the broth'—not if you read this book and follow Dan's example. Done right, collaboration is the key to harnessing the benefits of open innovation—be it on an individual, corporate, or even national level."

—**Martin Ihrig**
The Wharton School, University of Pennsylvania;
and I-Space Institute, LLC

"Every innovation stems from some external spark. The more you collaborate, the greater the chances of this happening. Dan gets this. Read this book and learn how you can MAKE this happen instead of waiting for it to happen TO YOU."

—**Matthew Graczyk**
CEO, Coupeez Inc.

"Dan lives by the rules of servant leadership that build the open, honest, and trusting foundation for collaboration. Sharing that in the book transforms his conduct into a world-changing pursuit."

—**Jeff Amerine**
Gravity Ventures

COLLABORATE

COLLABORATE

The Art of WE

Dan Sanker

JOSSEY-BASS
A Wiley Imprint
www.josseybass.com

Published by Jossey-Bass
A Wiley Imprint
One Montgomery Street, Suite 1200, San Francisco, CA 94104-4594—www.josseybass.com

Jossey-Bass books and products are available through most bookstores. To contact
Jossey-Bass directly call our Customer Care Department within the U.S. at 800-956-7739,
outside the U.S. at 317-572-3986, or fax 317-572-4002.

Wiley also publishes its books in a variety of electronic formats and by print-on-demand.
Some material included with standard print versions of this book may not be included
in e-books or in print-on-demand. If the version of this book that you purchased
references media such as CD or DVD that was not included in your purchase, you may
download this material at http://booksupport.wiley.com. For more information about
Wiley products, visit www.wiley.com.

Library of Congress Cataloging-in-Publication Data

Sanker, Dan, 1965–
    Collaborate : the art of we / Dan Sanker.
      p. cm.
    Includes bibliographical references and index.
    ISBN 978-1-118-11472-8 (cloth); 978-1-118-18055-6 (ebk.);
    978-1-118-18056-3 (ebk.); 978-1-118-18057-0 (ebk.)
      1. Strategic alliances (Business)   2. Teams in the workplace.
      3. Business networks.   4. Cooperativeness.   I. Title.
  HD69.S8S257   2012
  658.4'022—dc23

                          2011043161

Printed in the United States of America
FIRST EDITION
HB Printing   10 9 8 7 6 5 4 3 2 1

CONTENTS

To Jane, Julian, and Jon, for putting up with my endless hours on my laptop when I should have been doing something more fun. I think this topic will be important to my boys, our associates, our investors, our customers, our partners—and, frankly, to our society.

FOREWORD

As far as we know, this is the first book foreword to be written as a collaborative effort—possibly proving that Tom Clancy was wrong when he said, "Collaboration on a book is the ultimate unnatural act." A book foreword is usually an introductory section in which a "prominent person" discusses the author, the book, and the topic. From this book's title alone, a reader can infer that the author, Dan Sanker, believes that the prominence of any *individual* is dwarfed by the prominence of the *group*. As a result, he has used a creative approach: asking people who he believes have helped him become a better practitioner of the art of collaboration to collaboratively write the book's foreword. It was something of an example of what folks in the technology industry refer to as "dogfooding"—meaning "eating your own dog food," as when a company actually uses the products that it makes. Other, more elegant people have referred to it as "ice-creaming" or "drinking your own champagne." Regardless, the team's goal was to collaboratively deliver a foreword that discussed the usual topics that publishers in the industry suggest:

- The author's qualifications for writing the book

- The special contributions the book makes to the field

- The readers who will be interested in the book and why

- The ultimate significance of the book

Instead of the foreword being written by a great big muckety-muck, it has been developed in collaboration by a team using a wiki that the author popped up in about ten minutes.

It seems that most of us started with a somewhat negative impression of the highfalutin' concept of collaboration. We thought of many examples of times when we were part of insincere corporate efforts that started with the notion of empowerment. Some of these seemed more like phony empowerment. Workplace participation can mean a lot of things, but regrettably, the promise of democratic involvement in the workplace is all too often a disguise for the same old authoritarian institutional structures. Very few organizations actually allow associates to really shape meaningful matters of policy. As a result, employees who are promised participatory opportunities usually become disenchanted. The concept is great—an alternative to the dehumanizing concept of the division of labor wherein workers or individuals are treated like robots. But it has to go beyond giving lip service to the idea and be real.

Many people have seen their companies or organizations invest in the latest and greatest in collaboration gadgets and gizmos, but most still feel that nobody is getting much from collaboration efforts. There are tales of investment, rollouts, training, upgrading, meetings, and more to achieve the nirvana promised by the collaborative model. There are anecdotes about costly investments in Microsoft SharePoint servers and IBM QuickPlace applications that, at the end of the process, usually become solely the province of a select group of technorati. It's all enough to give the word "collaboration" a bad rep, along the lines of "We tried that once, but it seemed like waste of time." We've also seen collaborative exercises that *do* seem to generate some results, only to end up with some of the worst collaborators getting involved and derailing progress.

On the flip side, we all have this inherent sense that collaboration *is* one important key to innovation in the world we are currently living in. Throughout history we see the big bodacious ideas coming from collaborative efforts.

Any business leaders who use historical references as a guidepost for their own personal and professional development can easily see how collaboration has shaped our world. History does tend to repeat itself. For example, we considered some of the world's most influential people and found elements of collaboration almost everywhere that something actually worked. Would America exist as we know it without the Federalist Papers, which were created in collaboration among (as generally attributed) Alexander Hamilton, James Madison, and John Jay? The Federalist Papers are a series of eighty-five articles or essays promoting the ratification of the United States Constitution, without which the structure of America's founding papers would be substantially different.

Collaboration is the basis for much of the foundational arts and sciences. It is often speculated that Shakespeare, like most playwrights of his period, did not always write alone, and many of his plays are considered collaborative or were revised after their original composition. Leonardo Da Vinci made his sketches individually, but he collaborated with other people to flesh out the finer details. For example, his sketches of human anatomy were a collaboration with Marcantonio della Torre, an anatomist from the University of Pavia. Their collaboration is important because it marries the artist with the scientist. Similarly, Marie Curie's husband stopped his original research and joined Marie in hers. They went on to collaboratively discover radium, which overturned established ideas in physics and chemistry.

In the world of business, Jack Welch practiced collaboration at GE, championing the usefulness of constructive disagreement in reaching creative decisions. He had inherited a culture of what he called "superficial congeniality," in which people didn't tell each other the truth. Like Andy Grove at Intel, Welch recognized that conflict was inevitable in dealing with novel and complex decisions and that conflicting views contained information that needed to be harvested and incorporated into decisions. Before Grove and Welch, Lee Iacocca collaborated with designer Michael Leone and the Gaffoglio Family of metal crafters to customize what became known as "Iacocca Silver" Mustangs. Using the same collaborative method-ologies, Iacocca headed the Statue of Liberty-Ellis Island Foundation, which raised funds to renovate and preserve the Statue of Liberty.

Lou Gerstner is credited with turning IBM around in the 1990s. He described the turnaround as difficult and often wrenching for an IBM culture that had become insular and balkanized. He moved the culture in a more collaborative direction. The company is currently home to over 426,000 employees, with revenues approaching $100 billion and assets exceeding $113 billion. It is arguable whether IBM would still exist with-out Gerstner's collaborative changes.

Some have said that Oprah Winfrey may be the world's most powerful woman. But she didn't do it on her own. She has worked in collaboration on innumerable projects over her career. Oprah's Angel Network has raised over $80 million to improve access to education, protect basic rights, create communities of support, and empower people to become leaders. Even Nelson Mandela, himself an incredible collaboration champion, praised Winfrey for overcoming her disadvantaged youth to become a benefactor for others.

Rosa Parks is known for her act of defiance that became an important symbol of the modern civil rights movement. She collaborated with civil rights leaders, including Martin Luther King, Jr., helping launch him to national prominence. Without the collaborative beginnings of the civil rights movement, our society might not look anything like it does today.

Then there are the dramatic innovations that we all use every day. For example, many of you will be reading this book on a device that wouldn't exist without an early collaboration between Steve Jobs and Steve Wozniak. Wozniak's engineering talent and Jobs's ingenuity and marketing instincts started it all. Even the group writing this foreword used tools that wouldn't exist if Mark Zuckerberg hadn't formed the now-controversial collaboration with a few other important contributors in the early days of Facebook. And it is likely that none of us can go for long without using a search engine created in collaboration between Sergey Brin and Larry Page.

Dan's book opens the door for everyone to become an innovator. Dan introduces an idea that is much needed and will have a ripple effect in today's economic climate. Collaboration will help entrepreneurs get started, increase innovative technology, and help cut rising costs for everyone in the supply chain. The book allows readers to see every industry as a part of a whole. When two or more businesses put their cutthroat competitive ideals aside and come together, they can create new markets that could not have existed before.

Today's global economy is getting ever faster, and the way business is conducted must be as efficient as possible. This book is timely because collaboration is no longer just a good idea. It is absolutely essential for businesses to thrive and grow in this time of economic survival of the fittest. Each chapter helps takes "collaboration" from a nice word to a powerful growth strategy. In a most entertaining and persuasive fashion, Dan exposes the false choice between being a shrewd competitor and a community builder. This book turns the conventional idea of competition on its head: it's not about how many people you can defeat, but rather about how many people you can help win. It will shake the foundation of the business community. While most companies box it out in the same old ring, Dan shows us that the key to winning is lifting one another up. Dan and his book are definitive proof that collaboration is the only way to reach full potential, as a business, as a professional, and even as a human being. The real-life case studies presented here help us internalize how this kind of collaboration really works.

We all have a deep sense that collaborative environments deliver results. What we struggle with are ways to make collaboration a real and constructive thing in our organizations. The book is the tool that helps business leaders quickly and easily jump into game-changing mode and prepare themselves to capture tomorrow's business opportunities.

It is a real pleasure to see that Dan has captured a portion of his collaborative model and life experiences on paper for others to learn and grow from. His professional successes as an entrepreneur and leader in numerous organizations qualify him as an expert on the subject. As we have worked directly with Dan over the years, it's always been easy to leave each discussion motivated with a new perspective, renewed to try something innovative, and ready to face stubborn challenges. Now we've got the book!

Jeff Amerine

Robert Angstadt

Vatche Artinian

John F. Attanasio

Maggie Gorman Bell

Elizabeth K. Boch

Dan Borengasser

John Byrnes

Christopher Chomyn

Susan Gilliland Collier

Robert Decker

Greg B. Fleishman

Eric Freeman

Mark Goldstein

Matthew Graczyk

Carolyn Hughes

Kathryn Hunt-Miller

Dr. Martin Ihrig

Mark Jacobs

Steve Kampff

Abigail Kiefer

Dr. Thomas L. Lagö

Rich Lawrence

Jim Lollis

Kieron Loy

Michael D. Matteo, Jr.

Yasmine Omari

Shan Pesaru

Jim Phillips

Markita Rogers

Steven K. Rust

Damon Schechter

Michael Sevart

Jim Shankle

Aaron Stahl

Mark Stallcup

Kathryn Ullrich

Tom Verry

Eric Wolfe

Jay Wren

PREFACE

I was doing a guest lecture for an MBA class a few years ago when a student asked what I thought was *the* most important building block to a company's success. My initial answer was "People—finding great people." The student's facial reaction was probably a lot like mine when I was in business school and some gray-haired CEO said something just like that. *People—what?!*

I could tell by her expression that she thought it was an insincere answer (which it was not). She also asked what I thought was our company's competitive advantage, to which I responded, "The people, process, and technology to create collaborative solutions." All the students' facial expressions were pretty similar: *Collaboration—what?!* They brushed it off as a similarly insincere answer (which, again, it wasn't).

That began my writing project!

I am the CEO and founder of CaseStack, a full-service logistics company that offers warehousing, transportation, and an award-winning tech platform. We've been fortunate to win a lot of recognition over the years for being part of a select group with attributes including fastest-growing company, best place to work, best technology, greenest, and many more. And lots of people have been trying to figure out our secret sauce, so I thought I would try to take away the mystery: *collaboration* is that sauce. If you are like many of the people we have worked with over the years, you too may have a quizzical look on your face upon reading that word. Therein lies the reason for the book: too many quizzical looks on too many faces. That translates into too many lost opportunities.

It's my hope that this book makes my point. To put it in simple terms, collaboration is not some new-fangled idea, but it very much *is* newly important and enabled because of cultural and economic changes that are occurring related to technology and globalization. For the most part, we've all grown up and been trained in one primary business interaction methodology; competition. Ironically, my premise is that you will crush your competition if you develop and have access to another tool: collaboration.

Given that belief, it should come as no surprise that our company, CaseStack, is a successful experiment in collaboration. Ever since our founding in 1999, we have focused our efforts on collaboratively improving technology and customer-facing activities rather than making significant investments in buildings or trucks. More recently, even our hardware is cloud-based; that is, it resides on the Web rather than on our physical premises. Our cloud-based technology has been recognized many times for its ease of use, security, and functionality. Many of our key business partners could easily be misconstrued as competitors, but they are actually our closest allies. Our warehouse partners have integrated with us to the point that we often feel like we are the same company, and each partner has the highest certifications available in the industry. Our people work in their facilities; their people frequently use offices in ours. In addition, our most important service platforms have been developed with very large retailers who are not customers, vendors, or even partners in a legally documented sense; rather, they are co-collaborators. We'll talk more about this, but for now, suffice it to say we all have these common goals: cutting costs, increasing efficiency, and improving service. All parties are doing what they are best at, and in aggregate we are able to deliver at the lowest possible cost with the highest possible service quality. Through collaboration, we have built a completely non-asset-based company in a traditionally asset-heavy industry, and our growth has proven the concept successful. I hope that, in the pages ahead, you will discover the nuances and power of collaboration: *work with us and each other, and win.*

Acknowledgment

I want to extend a special thanks to Susan Gilliland Collier for all of her help in contemplating and developing my thoughts about collaboration and its vast opportunities.

INTRODUCTION

The world has not just turned upside down. It is turning every which way at an accelerating pace.

—TOM PETERS, THRIVING ON CHAOS

We usually look at business as a competitive game, a game like basketball, in which there is a winner and a loser. On a daily basis, business often feels like a war: one business lives and the other dies. Conquer, kill, and destroy your competitors. *The Art of War* by Sun Tzu is still considered timeless wisdom that applies as much to today's boardrooms as it did to a battle in the Chinese countryside back in the sixth century B.C. Not to say there is anything wrong with competition, but experienced managers ought to have more than one tool in the toolbox. True leaders use different tools for different situations; they can be trusted to rise to the occasion, whatever it may be, and make it work. Michael Jordan put it this way: "Talent wins games, but teamwork and intelligence wins championships."

Many view what has come to be called "social Darwinism" as a constant battle for survival—competition. Winners survive and losers disappear. But what that concept really describes is "survival of the winner," rather than Herbert Spencer's "survival of the fittest" or Darwin's true theory of natural selection. It is the extreme competitors who interpret "fittest" to be those who compete and "win." *In the coming decades, there is a strong case to be made that the fittest will be the ones who know how to collaborate. Great collaborators, ironically, will be the best competitors.* Collaboration with your customers, and sometimes even with apparent competitors, creates stronger businesses. Most important, collaboration often leads to the discovery of the biggest and best of innovations, the ones that address unknown latent opportunities (think of the iPhone, Swiffer, Post-it Notes, Netflix). While pure competitors are slugging it out—often anguishing over new ways to make the same mousetrap better, or ways to do the wrong things faster, better, and cheaper—there are collaborators in the wings actually innovating and finding solutions to problems many people didn't realize they even had.

We aren't talking about hackneyed concepts of win-win, synergy, or 1+1 = 3. We're talking about what Robert Wright wrote about in his book *Nonzero*, in which he shows that human culture has been evolving from tribes in barbaric competition to larger groups in civilized cooperation—moving toward more collaboration. According to Wright, in 1500 B.C. there were 600,000 autonomous political entities in the world; in the year 2000 there were only 195. Wright points out that in early cultures individuals, groups, tribes, chiefdoms, and states were constantly involved in zero-sum games. Nobody trusted anybody. Everybody assumed the worst about others. Fighting, treachery, slaughters, and wars were common. But we have managed to move beyond this to cooperation among towns, cities, counties, states, and many allied nations. Now, as Thomas Friedman so eloquently laid it out in his eponymous book, the world is flat, and we are moving at warp speed—together.

The key point to know is this: competition and collaboration are tools or styles; leaders must be prepared to use them at appropriate moments. In business school, everyone usually learns about the concept of situational management and situation leadership; that is, you don't succeed by always using the style you like the best. You use different management styles that are better suited to different situations, and you switch among them to maximize results. Similarly, the sole answer to all issues isn't always competition; sometimes a situation calls for collaboration to generate the biggest bang for the buck.

Seismic changes in technology, globalization, culture, and attitudes are occurring more quickly than ever. As we trek through our daily lives, it's difficult to go a day without being jolted by something dramatic that bumps up against our normal comfort zone. We run into new technology applications on a Friday that will change how we work on the following Monday. We see unraveling institutions that were so big that we did not comprehend that they could ever fail. We've begun to recognize that triple-A-rated financial instruments can be revealed to be junk within days, and seemingly solid industries or even countries may really be on the brink of bankruptcy. And we see these global issues actually affecting our personal lives and our career paths. Technology is changing how humans interact. Wealth is being destroyed and created more rapidly than ever before. According to the U.S. Department of Labor, younger baby boomers held an average of 10.8 jobs from ages eighteen to forty-two. Faced with all of this, many people are hunkering down, trying to get by in a new world that seems beset by increasing scarcity. But others are looking with curiosity at a new paradigm of the endless opportunities being created by collaboration.

Google Trends will tell you that the word "collaborate" is in searches twice as much as it was a few years ago; as of this writing, a search on "collaborate" yields about fifty-two million results. A lot of people are intrigued by this new paradigm in human interaction and the vastness of the opportunities that it might present. Many are talking about collaboration; some people are expounding the concept. Many think they are collaborating; others are really succeeding in doing so. This book is written for those with the drive and intellectual curiosity to try to step out from that world of seeming scarcity; to embrace a new way of thinking that requires a new approach to reach success. It is written to be read from beginning to end, starting with a description of collaboration—what it is and what it isn't. Then I discuss why now, more than ever, collaboration is doable and critical to success. There are examples of successes and failures to help readers identify the concept and the reasons for its importance. The middle of the book explains that although our traditional methodologies can be obstacles, we are each endowed with some natural collaborative instincts that can we can find and put into action. The final part of the book helps the reader understand the tactical requirements and use the tools to achieve collaborative success.

COLLABORATE

WHAT COLLABORATION IS AND ISN'T

None of us is as good as all of us.

—RAY KROC

We have become accustomed to the idea of winning through fierce competition. Simple concept: if you do something better than someone else, you win their market share. You eat their lunch. Collaborating with "competitors" is outside of our comfort zone; it seems alien and self-defeating. It feels as if we are helping "them" beat us at our own game.

We know successful competitors to be those who invest time, effort, and resources to win as big a piece of the pie as possible. The traditional wisdom holds that it is worth investing in these things to beat the competition, but the transaction costs of competing are high; higher than many realize. As traditional competitive business practices have evolved and spread deeper and wider throughout the world, and as new technology has made all competitors knowledgeable, there are diminishing marginal benefits available for the winners. The cost of stealing crumbs back and forth between competitors barely justifies the process as it whittles away at the small margin that does still exist. In many instances, collaboration will give us a greater return on our investment.

When successful collaborators invest time, effort, and resources, they capture a piece of pie that didn't exist before. Of the 765 CEOs surveyed in the IBM Global CEO Study 2006, 75 percent of respondents ranked collaboration as a "very important" part of innovation. The study also found higher revenue growth was reported by companies that collaborated with external resources than by those who did not (IBM Global Business Services, 2006). All parties increase their chance of success when they work together to create value that has never before existed. The old way of thinking traps competitors in a futile effort to steal pieces of an ever shrinking pie back and forth from each other; in the new way of thinking, collaborators are moving forward by working together to find ways to make the current pie larger or even to make an entirely new pie.

"Collaboration" is not a new buzzword to everyone. Over a decade ago Disney and McDonald's mastered the art of business collaboration and cross promotion. While waiting for Disney's release of a major new animated film, consumers of all ages knew that Happy Meal toys related to the movie as well as cross-promotional ads were on the way. The idea to form the relationship was brilliant and clearly a win-win for both organizations, because both companies are icons in America with built-in public goodwill. Although the Happy Meal probably needs another round of collaborative thought that involves advocacy groups, it still generates over $3 billion of annual revenue and represents about 20 percent of all McDonald's meals sold. Many companies do cross-promotion, but these two worked at a strategic level to attempt to increase each of their capabilities. They shared risks, rewards, and responsibilities by planning events before, during, and after a movie release. In addition, they have used movie advertising to sell food and food ads to sell more movies. The same principles apply for businesses seeking to grow or be more efficient in their business practices (Print Place Blog, 2009).

MUJI, a Japanese retailer, recently teamed up with legendary toy manufacturer LEGO to develop a product that adds an extra dimension to LEGO toys. If all MUJI did was make an add-on product that worked with LEGO, that could possibly be considered *cooperation*, but *collaboration* requires a high level of strategic work that can yield bigger results. In this case, MUJI and LEGO collaborated in the creation of a new series of toys that combine LEGO's plastic blocks with paper elements. The result: four play sets that feature a collection of redesigned LEGO parts, paper, and hole-punching tools that allow the user to combine them. Animals, characters, and a number of other shapes can be created using the sets, or they can be customized with a little imagination and additional paper (Robinson, 2009). Consider the effect on the two brands. MUJI is an award-winner for its simplistic design work; it sells a lot of ready-to-assemble furniture in its stores and seeks a creative and family-oriented image. LEGO's reputation for simplicity and family fun assembly complements the MUJI brand. LEGO reinforces its brand message that its designs are serious enough, yet simple enough, to be considered by a design leader like MUJI. Meanwhile, the new product receives increased exposure and sales in over 180 MUJI stores.

LEGO also collaborated with the UK shoe manufacturer Kickers to create a high-quality leather boot that is fun for children. This 2010 premium shoe collection uses the bright colors that typify the LEGO brand. The rubber trim on the Velcro version is an exact copy of a LEGO brick, so the child can attach an actual brick to the end of the straps, and a rubber fleurette is designed to be attached to the eyelets of the lace-up style. When the boots were first released, a free ticket to LEGOLand was included with each pair. And because Kickers is a stylish youth brand (created in 1968 in France), the association even gave LEGO some panache.

What Collaboration Is and What It Isn't

Collaboration is one of the popular business buzzwords of the moment, and companies are jumping on the bandwagon. Are they falling short of real collaboration and its benefits?

Collaboration is defined as the synergistic relationship formed when two or more entities working together produce something much greater than the sum of their individual abilities and contributions. Effective collaboration can produce better-quality projects, make more efficient teams, create healthier environments, greatly increase productivity, and enable more growth in organizations than ever could have existed before the concentrated emphasis was placed on collaboration. The business that quickly adopts a culture of collaboration will emerge stronger and more profitable than its counterparts that try to delay implementation of the collaboration required by the new knowledge-based economy. As Michael Schrage puts it in his book *Shared Minds*: ". . . collaboration is the process of shared creation: two or more individuals with complementary skills interacting to create a shared understanding that none had previously possessed or could have come to on their own." In a collaboration, multiple parties with complementary skills share knowledge, talents, skills, information, risks, and resources to achieve a mutual goal that they could not have achieved separately. The outcome of a successful collaboration is something that did not exist before: the solution to a problem; new ideas; a new, higher level of products, services, or know-how. Collaboration is not a touchy-feely concept; it's very much a focused, structured process.

To understand and master the power of collaboration, we need to be able to distinguish it from other, seemingly related forms of working with other people. Collaboration is more than simply sharing resources. We *work* with other people, but we do not *collaborate* when we simply post information about an upcoming visit by a prominent guest speaker, coordinate our activities with another agency to increase public awareness of a certain issue, or fund a university initiative for a river cleanup. Although networking, coordination, and cooperation—which all can be defined as different levels of resource sharing—offer certain benefits to at least one of the involved parties, each of them lacks one or more of the essential components of collaboration.

Resource Sharing: Just Part of Working Together

Resource sharing is a process that occurs at different stages of collaboration but does not, in itself, qualify as collaboration. Simple resource sharing takes place when we offer another party knowledge or information. For example, a friend may ask your advice on how to set up a new stereo system in his home because you have recently set up one for yourself. A professor may post on her office door a list of internship opportunities that her students could benefit from. Your company may allow another company to use your database in exchange for having access to theirs. All these are examples of simple resource sharing. At the end of such exchange, your friend may have the stereo system working, the professor's students may gain hands-on experience from the internships, and your organization may achieve its goals thanks to having access to an additional database. Yet none of these activities involves working together toward a common goal. None of them amounts to collaboration.

Apart from information and know-how, the resources in "resource sharing" can mean anything a business needs to operate (Business Dictionary, n.d.): financial resources, human capital, tangible resources (for example, equipment and technology), and intangible resources (for example, reputation and goodwill). Organizations and individuals engage in resource sharing for various reasons and with various goals in mind. Charity or altruistic reasons could be a factor. One could share resources with the intention of strengthening friendship or goodwill. Quid pro quo, or an exchange of tangible or intangible assets between parties, could also be a goal of resource sharing.

What makes simple sharing of resources different from collaboration? Lack of teamwork and absence of a unifying goal are the most obvious factors. In some cases, such as in charitable or altruistic sharing or acts of sharing out of friendship, only one of the parties can expect tangible benefits. As a result, simple resource sharing may fail to enhance the capacity of both parties. Finally, those involved in simple resource sharing are often more interested in the process than in the outcome. By contrast, a key feature of collaboration is that it is result-oriented, not process-oriented (Hansen, 2009).

To get a clearer picture, let's take a look at three forms of collective work that are related to collaboration but in fact represent three levels of resource sharing (Himmelman, 1993). These levels are networking, coordination, and cooperation.

Networking: A Start

Networking is defined as "the exchange of information or services among individuals, groups, or institutions," especially in order to cultivate productive business relationships (Merriam-Webster, n.d.). In simple terms, it is merely the act of sharing information for mutual benefit. Networking is a popular way of working with other people because it is relatively simple to do and it promises mutual benefit to all involved. It is also the most informal and noncommittal way of working with other people, compared to three C's: coordination, cooperation, and collaboration. Networking is often the first step toward collaboration.

Networking usually involves communicating and working with people who have interests similar to ours. For example, organizations and individuals concerned about the ethical aspect of pollution may decide to set up a mailing list to share new information and organize regular meetings to discuss the issue. A software developer may attend a large IT conference to evaluate market trends and see whether the project she has in mind could attract interest from big IT businesses.

Networking is easy to do because we have a wide pool of potential networking activities at our disposal, ranging from talking with our neighbors to attending professional meetings and conferences (The Riley Guide, n.d.). In fact, we network every day. We are networking when we make new acquaintances at a party, chat with a local shopkeeper, join social clubs or religious groups, contribute to mailing lists and blogs, or post messages in chat rooms. Nearly everyone today, even outside of a business environment, is aware of the unequivocal benefits of networking. We often discover new ideas, business opportunities, or new ways of potential career development thanks to active networking.

Networking is informal; it does not require official meetings and organizational involvement. It can be done over a dinner or a couple of drinks, and you can walk out of a networking event whenever you please. Networking is a noncommittal activity. It is also an act of simple sharing of resources, not true collaboration. That said, networking is often a first step toward identifying a collaborative opportunity.

Coordination: Taking It to a Higher Level

More formal and somewhat more complex than networking, coordination means synchronization and integration of activities, responsibilities, and control to ensure the most efficient use of resources in order to achieve specified objectives (Business Dictionary). In simple terms, coordination requires that some action be taken and that there is a sharing of information for mutual benefit and to achieve a common goal. Coordination is an integral part of collaboration, but it cannot be a substitute for it.

Because coordination is a way to achieve a specific purpose, it calls for a more organizational approach than networking. It requires a higher level of involvement and responsibility from its participants. Coordination is an important part of public awareness campaigns and grassroots movements, especially those that call for a certain action or demand specific changes in the status quo. For example, various groups and organizations working in an undeveloped country may decide to have an AIDS awareness week, showing educational films, giving out red ribbons, and organizing a marathon to draw people's attention to the issue. Parents and teachers in a small town may draft a schedule so that two adults always accompany children who walk to school in areas where the school bus does not run.

Coordination is most successful when parties affected by the proposed changes can contribute to the discussion of those changes. This method of working with other people creates a wealth of ideas, ensures awareness of different views on the consequences of one's actions, and enables broader participation from various groups. It is effective in preventing duplication of efforts and helps to promote the common cause.

However, despite offering the same goal for the parties involved, coordination falls short of collaboration. Distinct groups working toward the same cause usually walk away from the coordination process as distinct groups. All parties work independently from each other, merely doing so at the same time as the other groups. Their learning from each other is limited. Finally contrast the best result of coordination—achieving a previously identified goal—with the best result of collaboration: attaining a new, higher level of products, services, or know-how.

Cooperation: Even More Significant

Cooperation means a "voluntary arrangement in which two or more entities engage in a mutually beneficial exchange instead of competing" (Business Dictionary). In simple terms, it combines the attributes of coordination with the sharing of resources. Thus, in addition to exchanging knowledge and synchronizing or adapting activities to achieve a common goal, cooperation includes the additional element of sharing business resources other than information. As part of cooperation, we may share funding, training, employees, workspace, marketing, and legal advice (Himmelman, 1993). Franklin D. Roosevelt famously said, "Competition has been shown to be useful up to a certain point and no further, but cooperation, which is the thing we must strive for today, begins where competition leaves off."

Although having a common goal is typical for cooperating parties, the degrees of their attachment to that goal may differ. Although crucial for one of the parties, a common project may be less important—or a mere issue of status—to the other party (Saveri, n.d.). In this case, the latter party learns little from the experience and does not evolve. Cooperation therefore falls short of collaboration for the following reasons: Although both cooperating parties may achieve their common goal, they do not necessarily enhance each other's capacity. In addition, cooperating parties do not fully share risks, responsibilities, and rewards. In the case of collaboration, all available resources, as well as risks, responsibilities, and rewards, are fully shared.

Consider this example. In 2006, two businessmen from Chicago developed a design contest website, Crowdspring.com, which enables graphic designers to get input from the entire community (Steiner, 2009). The idea is simple: companies and other potential clients offer to host a contest for the best logo, ad flier, or business card design, and designers submit their work to this contest, at the same time critiquing the work of others and exchanging comments and feedback. Because all designers participating in the project share the same goal—namely, to provide the client with the best logo, banner, or other design product—Crowdspring may resemble a collaborative tool. However, it is not. One glance at the components of collaboration tells us the Crowdspring model has more elements of competition than collaboration. Indeed, at the end of the day, the designers work independently and compete with each other for the prize. Collaboration, in contrast, is about working together as a team, building on each other's work, proposing and assessing new creative ideas, and communicating with each other in an open and respectful environment. Collaboration is about the common goal of the team, not individual goals of its members.

The CaseStack Collaboration Experience: A Case Study

CaseStack is often broadly characterized as a technology-enabled supply chain business process outsourcing company, but most customers would describe it more specifically as a third-party logistics company that offers warehousing and transportation services with a technology package that seamlessly ties it all together. Clients usually appreciate that they have tapped into high-quality services at lower costs, and that they have full reporting and visibility from their laptops or mobile devices anywhere, anytime. They don't really need to recognize, nor do they need to even think about, the higher vision. It is just critical to them that the service consistently performs at a higher rate and the costs are low enough to level the playing field in the highly competitive consumer packaged goods market.

But there *is* a higher vision. An allegory comes to mind. In sixteenth-century Italy, a church was being built, and three bricklayers were each asked the same simple question: "What are you doing?" The first bricklayer responded, "I am a bricklayer, and I am laying bricks. That's my job." The second bricklayer responded, "I am helping to build a big new building." The third had a completely different notion of the greater vision. He responded, "I am building an edifice to God that will bring people closer to a higher power."

The CaseStack vision is by no means as grandiose as the message conveyed by the third bricklayer, but it recognizes that there is a higher calling. The company was founded on the concept of developing a unique group of people, processes, and technology that could be leveraged to create collaborative relationships that would change the industry. This was based on the belief that the largest opportunities for business growth were often missed at traditional companies. Over the generations, companies have become very good at exploiting internal opportunities, sometimes using third-party resources. Many successful institutions are built to rally their organizations to compete, but they often miss out on collaborative opportunities. CaseStack obviously requires a strong competitive framework, but it also has a unique perception of collaboration. As an organization, its people, processes, and technology are conditioned to seek opportunities that span beyond the four walls. They are constantly in search of innovation based on collaboration; working between organizations as well as within. In a world where people tend to focus on scarcity and lack of opportunity, CaseStack has always faced a different quandary—too much opportunity. Though it may sound like an embarrassment of riches, culling through, evaluating, and developing the most promising from such a pool is still a challenging task.

Advertising executive David Ogilvy, who is often referred to as the father of advertising, said, "Ninety-nine percent of advertising doesn't sell much of anything." Unfortunately, there is no way to identify which 1 percent *will* be successful, so every possible avenue must be pursued. Innovative collaborative opportunities are much the same. There is no way of knowing which will pay off, so every viable possibility requires some exploration. It requires more forward thinking than what we are accustomed to, but as with advertising, when pursuing an opportunity leads to a gold strike, the payoff is clear. Advertisers have realized this with such advertising gems as "I've fallen, and I can't get up!" "Where's the beef?" and "Got milk?" These strokes of brilliance exemplify the concept that Ogilvy cites. And so it is with collaboration. Finding the mutually beneficial needle in the haystack with other organizations has become part of the CaseStack culture.

Some companies are much more fortunate in the percentage of successes, though they aren't the norm. There are companies out there that can do no wrong; they've found what could be called an *unfair* competitive advantage. They've got it made. They have monopoly power based on their dominance of a market, patent protection, indecipherable intellectual property, or unshakeable consumer loyalty (think Nutella, LEGO, Monty Python, Pabst beer, Trader Joe's, Birkenstock, Dr. Seuss). CaseStack is more of an example of a company that has to compete every day based on inherent market demands for *better, cheaper, faster*. That's what should make the company interesting as a case study; its collaborative tools are usable at most companies that compete in a normal business paradigm. We have developed a unique group of people, process, and technology that combine to give us a competitive edge and likely make us the most scalable company in our industry. The following examples will give some insights into how CaseStack collaborates.

CaseStack's Retailer Consolidation Program

One of the most notable collaborative programs that CaseStack has pioneered is its use of retailer-driven consolidation programs. In a normal environment, many consumer packaged goods companies use time-honored methods to fulfill orders from retailers from their warehouses. In simple terms, a purchase order comes in, the supplier stages the products on pallets, and they contact a trucker to deliver it to the retailer. Often that shipment does not completely fill a truck, so they use less-than-truckload services or partial trucks; either method means more wasted miles, time, and diesel fuel, and more greenhouse gas emissions.

In collaboration with large retailers, CaseStack cultivated something very different called *retailer-driven consolidation*. By developing technology and processes with retailers, CaseStack facilitates ordering and consolidation of multisupplier full truckloads. So, again in simple terms: the orders for numerous different products from distinct, unrelated companies come as one. Then they are shipped out on full trucks together. Transportation costs less, fewer resources are wasted, on-time delivery is higher, and even the Earth's environment is better off. Retailers get exactly what they need when they need it, reducing inventory carrying costs. Without the program, retailers would need to order larger quantities; now they can order as little as one case, but enjoy the benefits of full truckload consolidated pricing. In addition, the average CaseStack truck is carrying sixteen loads, so a single truck can replace up to sixteen separate trucks pulling into the retailers' distribution yards. That reduces operating expenses. Many mid-sized suppliers have actually stated that they might have gone out of business without such a program, and retailers have benefitted by being able to add variety to their shelves.

All of this couldn't have happened without a lot of collaboration. Each party went out on a limb in the beginning: the retailers, the suppliers, and CaseStack. Each invested time, some invested capital, and all risked sharing closely guarded information, knowledge, and processes with each other for the greater good. The savings achieved by the collaboration are passed through the entire supply chain—from the manufacturer to the retailer and finally to the consumer. At the end of the day, just like the third bricklayer in the Italian church allegory, we achieved something sensational: lower costs for the mother on a tight budget in the grocery store buying food for her family. No individual party in the process could have achieved this alone. This example has become an important part of CaseStack's business model, but the company leverages collaborative practices in innumerable other ways.

The "VIVA Consumer" Example

As part of the CaseStack collaborative business model, we often have strategy meetings with retailers, consumer goods companies, and other supply chain participants to determine future trends. One trend that we have recently discussed relates to changing consumer expectations and the consequential requirements for a more contemporary supply chain. During the collaborative process, we first perceived only a small part of the opportunity as simply the convergence of business-to-business (B2B) and business-to-consumer (B2C) retailing models. B2B describes commerce transactions between businesses, such as between a manufacturer and a wholesaler or between a wholesaler and a retailer. B2C, sometimes also called business-to-customer, describes activities of businesses serving end consumers with products and/or services. A manufacturer that sells its products to Tesco or Walmart is selling B2B, whereas the eBay, Tmall, or Amazon model is more likely B2C. Most consumers already realize that B2B and B2C are converging. For example, what is happening when a shopper is standing in a Costco building using her mobile device to purchase a less expensive version of some product online at Walmart.com that will be shipped to and available at the FedEx office nearby her house for pickup later that week? It's a convergence of B2B and B2C. The lines that define the structure of retail are blurring.

As we worked collaboratively with various partners on the convergence issue, we began to understand the larger trend. Global consumer expectations are evolving; we are seeing what we have dubbed a new "VIVA Consumer" that demands a "VIVA Supply Chain." VIVA is our acronym for Variety, Instantly, Value, and Anywhere. In more conventional terminology it refers to the reality that consumers are beginning to expect that they can have full product assortment (variety), any time they feel like it (instantly), at the usual prices (value), and available wherever they happen to want it (anywhere). Most industry participants recognize that traditional supply chains in the United States and elsewhere weren't actually developed to accommodate the reality of the VIVA Consumer, and creating it will require significant expertise, scale, and scope that only collaboration can deliver. We wouldn't have properly understood the extent of the larger opportunity ourselves without the deep and varied talents of our collaborative partners.

We used our collaborative model to understand the opportunity, and then we started taking the first steps to address the issue. For example, CaseStack has focused primarily on business-to-business (B2B) logistics, less on business-to-consumer (B2C) services. As a result of the changing marketplace, we realize that we will require a greater array of services. It makes sense for CaseStack to offer B2C services that are equally as progressive as its B2B services. In response to this new opportunity, CaseStack began collaborating with a technology-oriented B2C industry leader. As it turns out, given the developing marketplace convergence, the B2C company had a "mirror image" opportunity for its clients, who were increasingly requiring more B2B services. Like any collaborative relationship, it started with a problem to solve or an idea for something bigger and better. It required companies to meet and share information for mutual benefit to achieve a common goal. Both shared resources and took action to increase their mutual capabilities even in the face of risks. Each aims to be the best in its field for full logistics services from B2C through B2B—soup to nuts. There are many other parts that will come together to develop a comprehensive solution for the much larger opportunity, but we have begun building part of the foundation.

Leveraging Competitor and Customer Relationships

Most companies like CaseStack would normally consider others in the logistics business as competitors. There are a host of logistics companies that aggregate to about $1 trillion in business each year. Examples of large companies in the industry include Fedex, UPS, C.H. Robinson, and even the U.S. Postal Service. In another collaborative effort, CaseStack is working with some industry players to design mutually beneficial programs to leverage each company's strengths in collaboration. Each relationship requires a certain level of intellectual curiosity and initiative to get started. Usually that starts with a simple call, followed by an introductory meeting. As each firm gets to know the other's strengths, weaknesses, opportunities, and threats, they can begin to engage in a long-term, trust-based business partnership. In the case of the logistics companies, CaseStack and its newfound partners are designing specific tools, technology, and processes to leverage each other's strengths. As a result, overall costs are lower and each company is more competitive. This same principle is currently working with certain CaseStack customers as well. For example, CaseStack has long provided shipping services for an animal health and equipment products company. This animal products company also uses some of its own fleet of trucks. In many cases those trucks return from stores back to this company's twenty-six warehouses completely empty; in the industry this is known as "empty backhaul." Through a collaborative program, CaseStack is working closely with the client to use those otherwise empty truck miles for other customers' shipments. CaseStack receives low-cost, high-quality trucking services, and the customer transforms its truck fleet from a cost center to a profit center.

Other Collaborative Programs

There is a diverse range of programs, from mission-critical to merely community service–oriented, wherein CaseStack leverages its well-developed platform to act as a catalyst for mutually beneficial opportunities. For example, the company has collaborated with universities, nongovernmental organizations (NGOs), and state entities to assist in the development of SphereAccess, an organization that connects retail buyers with international suppliers. CaseStack also played an instrumental role in the creation and maturation of Green Valley Development, a non-profit coalition that fosters collaboration and commercialization of sustainability technology. CaseStack was even able to apply its collaborative skills to assemble a response team in the wake of the 2011 tornado in Joplin, Missouri, to assist the Missouri State Jobs Commission help recently unemployed victims get back on their feet.

There are numerous other collaborative ventures that rely on each part of the collaboration continuum—from sharing information and resources for mutual benefit in pursuit of common goals to taking action—all to increase mutual capabilities, even in the face of complexities regarding shared risks, rewards, and responsibilities. They all start with introductory relationship building and work their way toward strategic congruency to achieve new innovative solutions.

Real Collaboration

Collaboration is a process that can be broken down into its essential components. As with coordination, some action is taken and information is shared for mutual benefit and to achieve a common goal. As in cooperative arrangements, resources are shared. But a collaborative exercise is much more strategic, requiring the parties to increase each other's capabilities, and all take on some shared risks, rewards, and responsibilities.

As we have seen in this chapter, simple resource sharing is not collaboration; nor are its more advanced levels of networking, coordination, and cooperation. All these ways of working with other people can be beneficial to at least one of the parties involved. The goals may diverge, however, and responsibilities, risks, and rewards are not shared by all members of the process.

For true collaboration, the parties need a higher level of commitment, a unifying goal, and a structure to enable group communication, group participation, brainstorming, and teamwork, all of which come together to achieve something far greater than would otherwise be possible.

2

DAWN OF THE KNOWLEDGE-BASED COLLABORATIVE ERA

It is not the strongest of the species that survive, nor the most intelligent, but the one most responsive to change.

—CHARLES DARWIN

What comes to mind when you think of the term "survival of the fittest"? You might imagine a competitive battle for survival, in which winners survive and losers disappear. Yet in the coming decades, as we continue to move from an information-based to a knowledge-based economy, there is a strong case to be made that the fittest will be not the ones who have the greatest ability to simply compete, but those who are best able to collaborate as well.

Throughout modern society, collaborations are becoming a business imperative. According to Frances Westley and Harriet Vredenburg of McGill University, "Partnerships, strategic alliances, and interfirm networks have been viewed as critical structural innovations designed to address the kinds of ill-defined problems that depend on multiple perspectives and resources for their solution" (Westley & Vredenburg, 1997, p. 381). The reality is that while traditional companies continue to cannibalize their own margins by fighting over market share, collaborative organizations are creating new markets and growing the size of the overall market. In fact, according to a 2006 study by Frost & Sullivan, sponsored by Microsoft and Verizon Business, collaboration is one of the key driving factors behind a company's performance. The study found that the impact of collaboration "is twice as significant as a company's aggressiveness in pursuing new market opportunities (strategic orientation) and five times as significant as the external market environment (market turbulence)" (Microsoft, 2006). (For more about this study, see Chapter Three.)

Where We've Been: From Industrial Revolution to Information Economy

To understand why collaboration has become so essential today, we need to review a little history. The industrial revolution of the mid- to late 1700s and 1800s, which brought about machine-based manufacturing and improvements in transportation, shaped our economy until the middle of the twentieth century. Innovation and technological advances that forever changed the production, distribution, and consumption of goods helped us create millions of jobs and made the United States a world leader in producing innovative, high-quality products and processes, including assembly-line production, the telegraph, automobiles, and pharmaceuticals. In that economy, companies succeeded by investing in research and design and by fine-tuning the art of competition.

But then things began to change. As the country's economy has matured, it has gone through transitional phases, placing more and more value on intellectual capital and less on physical labor. Just as the agricultural economy gave way to the Industrial Revolution, the importance of manufacturing and the time devoted to it declined, while information and service industries became more vital in providing products and service. The industrial economy that brought so much prosperity to so many people began shifting to what many people call the information economy. According to the online Business Dictionary, the information economy was (and still is) characterized by three things: "(1) the convergence and integration of communication and data processing technologies into information technology (IT), (2) the pervasive influence of IT on economic activity, such that most workers are information workers and most products are information products, and (3) application of IT networks throughout the economic institutions, organizations, and processes, resulting in a very high degree of flexibility, weakening of regulatory control, and acceleration of globalization."

Economist and entrepreneur Marc Porat, who created foundational measures of the information economy within his nine-volume doctoral dissertation at Stanford University and went on to work for the U.S. Department of Commerce, says that an economy becomes an information economy when information-related work begins to exceed work related to the other sectors. That had happened, says Porat, by 1967, when 53 percent of the U.S. workforce was engaged in "information work" (Porat, 1977).

During the last half of the twentieth century, the information era completely changed the way in which day-to-day business was conducted in this country and around the world, giving rise to revolutionary improvements to existing products and processes as well as the creation of new ones that we could not have imagined previously and that we can no longer imagine how we ever did without. AMC's hit television show *Mad Men* reminded us that photocopying machines amazed and delighted office workers of the early 1960s; by the 1980s, businesses were using fax machines to exchange documents instantly; by the turn of the twenty-first century, technology such as e-mail and instant messaging was allowing us to communicate rapidly without having to track people down by phone, and virtual meeting websites were increasing our productivity by freeing up time and money previously spent on travel.

Where We're Going: The Knowledge-Based Economy

Now things are changing again. The information economy of the late twentieth century is rapidly giving way to the knowledge-based economy of the twenty-first. Financial capital is being replaced by intellectual capital as the driver that enables business to grow, and innovative knowledge-based firms, instead of the large industrial firms of the not-so-distant past, are now leading the way.

The new knowledge-based economy requires more than simply acquiring and storing information; having knowledge means that we can understand that information and apply it in a useful manner. For example, a teenager can read a how-to wiki to get information about how to drive a car. She might even memorize all of the steps. However, if she is asked whether she knows how to drive a car after simply reading about it online, the correct answer is "no." She has the information that will enable her to gain knowledge, but she does not yet have the actual knowledge that comes from doing. Similarly, a call center employee who uses a database to answer customers' questions is relying on currently available information that can be accessed and relayed to the caller. But in order to work with customers to identify problems and come up with solutions, he also needs to use his experience, expertise, and analytical skills.

With the Internet, we all have access to huge amounts of information, but that access alone doesn't make us truly knowledgeable about anything. In a business environment, we see the difference every day—people have the information they need, and they may even have training in how to do something, yet they just can't get the job done. What they need is more of the knowledge that comes from actually putting the information to work.

The implications of this shift from an information-based to a knowledge-based economy are profound. Although information—which can be collected, stored, and made available for use as needed—is often the visible product, knowledge in this emerging economy has genuine value. As such, it is quickly becoming an organization's most important asset. Wealth in the industrial era came from leveraging assets such as machines and property, but wealth in the knowledge-based economy is generated by using the education, experience, and intelligence of human capital. It is by making the best possible strategic allocation of its people's knowledge that an organization gains a real competitive advantage over its less innovative competitors. Winners in society will tap the Earth's best and brightest through collaborative practices.

The New Economy Demands Innovation

The transition from an information-based to a knowledge-based economy requires more than a better marketing strategy, a system upgrade, or a new software package. Business today moves too quickly for routine fixes. The time it takes to go from idea to market is getting shorter, and change happens quickly and often. To survive, organizations must be able to innovate so they can solve intractable problems, come up with new products and services, and constantly adapt to new developments.

In short, success in this new economy demands the kind and quality of innovation that results from collaboration, which brings together a diversity of information, knowledge, skills, and perspectives to create something altogether new. In fact, when people are sharing knowledge and working toward a common goal, they often discover needs that were unknown until the means to fulfill the need was created.

Henry Ford said it well: "If I'd asked my customers what they wanted, they would have said a faster horse." Like Steve Jobs in our own era, Henry Ford understood that consumers have latent needs—needs they may not realize they have. In Ford's case, the consumer was thinking *horse*, but Ford had already innovated beyond their expectations. That kind of innovation in the technology industry has given us iPods, smart phones, tablets, and more. According to Rich Jaroslovsky, writing on technology for the *San Francisco Chronicle*, "[T]he entire consumer industry is based on selling people stuff they didn't know they wanted or needed" (Jaroslovsky, 2011).

A great many popular innovations were actually the result of collaborations that began informally, with people talking to one another about a shared interest or concern. As Charles Leadbeater, British author and former advisor to Tony Blair, pointed out in a speech at a 2005 TED conference, the mountain bike resulted not from the work of a genius working alone in his cubicle. The idea originated with consumers who were sharing their frustrations with the limitations of traditional racing bikes as they rode the mountain trails of Marin County. As Leadbeater mentioned, nobody could have known during the early stages that thirty years later, mountain bikes and mountain bike equipment would account for 65 percent of bike sales in the United States (Leadbeater, 2005).

Further, as anyone who has seen the film *The Social Network* knows, Facebook began life as a website that let Harvard college students post photos of "hot" women. Even when it was redesigned and found success as a social networking tool for college students, it is likely that no one could have predicted that it would go on to play a powerful role in cultural change and global politics. Although you may leave the film with the impression of Mark Zuckerberg as a lone wolf, when he first conceived of Facebook he collaborated with other Harvard computer science students—Chris Hughes, Eduardo Saverin, and Dustin Moskovitz—to draw up the source code and collaborate on a design.

Similarly, Procter & Gamble (P&G) seemed unlikely to enter the plastic wrap business, but a promising plastic film technology discovered through diaper research paved the way for one of P&G's best external partnerships. The plastic wrap now known as Glad Press'n Seal resulted from an innovation developed and successfully test marketed by P&G. However, the company decided that it would not be prudent to be a novice in such a well-established category. Instead, it formed a joint venture with Clorox, one of its biggest competitors in the cleaning products sector, which already had strong brand equity and the leading plastic wrap: Glad.

Both P&G and Clorox invested significantly in the joint venture when it was formed in 2002. P&G contributed the intellectual property behind Press'n Seal as well as future innovations, including the technology behind the revolutionary Glad ForceFlex trash bags (introduced two years later). P&G also contributed global marketing expertise. Clorox brought its R&D expertise in resins, its brand equity in the plastic bags and wrap categories, and the organizational structure for creating and distributing new plastic film products.

Total Glad sales doubled in the four years after the joint venture was formed, making Glad a billion-dollar brand. The Glad joint venture allowed P&G and Clorox to collaboratively work together to build a bigger business than each could have developed on its own. Meanwhile, each still protects the integrity of its parent company, and every day each battles it out with its collaborative partner in other categories (Procter & Gamble, n.d.).

A Bigger Piece of the Pie—Or an Entirely New Pie

The traditional wisdom holds that successful businesses are those that invest time, effort, and resources in the competitive process to win as big a piece of the pie as possible. It's true that the ability to compete remains an important tool for organizational success. But the transaction costs of competing are high—higher, in fact, than many people realize. As traditional competitive business practices have evolved and spread deeper and wider throughout the world, and as new technology has made all competitors knowledgeable, there are diminishing marginal benefits available for the winners.

What happens when companies stop competing for crumbs of an existing pie and instead focus on getting a good-sized piece of a larger—or entirely new—pie? When businesses invest time, effort, and resources in collaboration instead of competition, they are likely to gain a piece of pie that didn't exist before. That was the finding of an IBM study: higher revenue growth was reported by companies that collaborated with external resources than by those who did not (IBM Global Business Services, 2006).

Increasingly, the competitive advantage will go to those companies that create a diverse network of partners around the globe from which they can draw a wealth of knowledge. Both individuals and organizations increase their chance of success when they work together to come up with innovative solutions to problems and create value that has never before existed.

The best business models of the twenty-first century rely on collaboration instead of cutthroat competition. In fact, the traditional all-out competitive model doesn't always perform as intended. For example, while car companies are battling it out for market share, they are having a difficult time collaborating within their own dealer networks. A recent report indicates that car manufacturers are encountering competition for their ad slots, and that competition is coming from none other than their brand's competing car dealerships. Instead of joining forces to make the best use of their and their dealers' limited advertising resources, car companies are allowing dealers to use their ad dollars to compete against the dealer down the street. If the car companies were to collaborate with their own dealers, both parties could pool their limited money to focus on their brand—not on which dealer is better. Instead of a Ford dealer using ad money to beat up another Ford dealer, the money could be used to promote Ford as better than Chrysler, GM, Toyota, or Nissan.

Yet ad spending by dealers has increased dramatically over the last two years, and the increase has resulted in bidding wars on third-party sites like Edmunds.com and Cars.com. In 2007, online ad spending by car dealerships was up to $32 million, and that figure has more than doubled each year since 2005. Online ad pricing is measured in cost per thousand impressions (CPM)—and an ad spot that came with a $4 CPM price tag two years ago now costs $34. Advertising profits for Edmunds.com went up 64 percent in 2006 and another 93 percent in 2007. Although the third-party websites are clearly the winners in this exercise, the loser is the brand identity. With so many voices trying to tell the same story and sell the same product, the carefully crafted message designed by the original equipment manufacturers can easily become diluted and confused (Adam, 2008).

Success in the Global Economy

One of the key forces propelling the new economy forward is globalization. Trade, finance, R&D, and communication are becoming more and more integrated, and geographic boundaries are disappearing as technology advances and businesses become more interdependent. The driver of this change is technology.

In the old industrial economy, the lack of sufficient technology kept the competition limited to a local level. Today, rapid advances in communication-related technology mean that people around the world are now using common tools that offer them ready access to one another. At the same time, there is an increasing movement toward global standardization. U.S. accounting standards are moving toward international standards, multinational companies are assembling teams around product lines instead of countries, and employees are increasingly experiencing stints in other countries.

We are becoming more the same as we use similar technology tools with similar content every day—as of this writing, there are six hundred million people on Facebook, and Twitter and Google are ubiquitous, helping us to become a global workforce and marketplace. As a result, businesses now operate in a hypercompetitive global environment in which the game is constantly changing. It is becoming more and more difficult—even impossible—for companies working alone to hold onto a competitive advantage for long (Hypercompetition: Financial Times Lexicon, n.d.). When kids graduate with their fresh new college diplomas, they need to realize that they are now part of a global pool of 6.9 billion people, and according to a study by Harvard and the Asian Development Bank, 6.7 percent of the world's population are college degree holders. That's up from 5.9 percent in 2000. Graduates need to realize how competitive the job market has become.

To survive and prosper in this global economy, organizations need to find ways of increasing their ability to compete, which often means expanding into new, well-populated markets. There are countless examples of American corporations that are expanding outside the United States to tap into the greater growth potential of emerging economies around the world.

However, conducting business in emerging economies can be highly challenging—and unpredictable. To meet the challenges, many companies are collaborating with local partners on various aspects of their growth strategies. The Las Vegas Sands Corporation, which operates the Venetian

Macao, had $3.3 billion in net revenue in Macau in 2009, about three times the revenue of its Vegas properties. The LVS 10-Q filed on August 9, 2011 shows that the total casino revenues in the Macao properties were ten times that of the Las Vegas properties (Edgar SEC Filings 2011).

Wal-Mart Stores, Inc., operates under many different international brands in sixteen countries. The company has a large presence in Japan, and it has opened over 300 stores in China. It has overcome some owner-ship obstacles in India through collaboration with Delhi-based conglom-erate Bharti Enterprises. In August 2007, Walmart announced an agreement with Bharti to establish a joint venture, Bharti Walmart Private Limited, for wholesale cash-and-carry and back-end supply chain management operations in India (Sharma, 2011).

Other American companies are also looking to the international market to expand their pool of potential customers. In China alone, the long list of organizations that are working jointly with local companies includes AIG, Beatrice Foods, Brown & Root, P&G, Squibb, and United Technologies.

In a specific mutually beneficial example, in 2008 Sun Microsystems (acquired by Oracle in 2010) and China's Ministry of Education (MOE) launched a three-year collaboration agreement designed to help China meet its demand for cultivating integrated circuit (IC) engineering talent and industry development. The agreement was based on Sun's OpenSPARC program, which China selected because Sun is the only major vendor to freely offer its designs to the open source community and because it makes the fastest microprocessor in the world.

As a result of the agreement, China can educate students on the latest processor innovations. Because the curriculum is based on Sun's open archi-tecture, students are empowered to accelerate innovation on top of the OpenSPARC design. Sun CEO Jonathan Schwartz called the collaboration "a launching point for similar relationships with economies and universities worldwide, and an unmistakable endorsement of Sun's open source approach to building opportunity across software, systems and microelectronics."

Professor Zhao Qinping, vice minister of MOE, said, "We appreciate Sun's open source strategy, especially Sun's outstanding contribution in the open-sourced IC area, and we encourage the active cooperation effort between China's universities and Sun in the teaching and research area. We believe the cooperation will be beneficial in advancing China's teaching and research level in the IC area" (HPC Wire, 2008).

Whereas traditional business theory would have led companies attempting to do business overseas to use their muscle to gain market share, these firms and the many other firms now doing business in other countries have chosen to make strong local connections with already established local powerhouses. Instead of competing against these established brands, they have made the strategic decision to cooperate and collaborate for mutual benefit, thus gaining access to large, rapidly growing markets that they most likely would not have been able to enter as quickly on their own.

If You Can't Beat 'Em, Join 'Em

In the *Harvard Business Review*, authors Larry Huston and Nabil Sakkab (2006) described what they call the "connect and develop model" that Procter & Gamble used when its executives realized that they could not afford to try to keep growing "by spending greater and greater amounts on R&D for smaller and smaller payoffs." Under the new model, P&G "collaborates with suppliers, competitors, scientists, entrepreneurs and others. Outsiders who were traditionally shunned at P&G are more welcomed. Procter systematically scours the Earth for proven intellectual property, packages, and products that P&G can improve, scale up, and market (in other words, commercialize)." P&G executives decided on this model when they keenly observed that "for every P&G researcher there were 200 scientists or engineers elsewhere in the world who were just as good—a total of perhaps 1.5 million people whose talents we could potentially use." In the first two years after implementing the new model, P&G launched more than a hundred new items and experienced a productivity increase in its R&D division of almost 60 percent.

Internal Collaboration

Although the benefits are substantial, collaboration with other organizations, especially competitors, can be complex and pose some risks (more on this in Chapter Four). The workplace seems to be a more logical place for collaboration to take place. Unfortunately, many organizations fail to encourage collaboration among their employees, and many corporate cultures actively discourage it or fail to provide the support that is essential for it to succeed.

That's surprising, when you consider that collaboration among the various teams and departments is central to an organization's ability to make the best use of its resources, increase its productivity, and succeed in today's crowded marketplace. But most people and organizations have a tendency to continue doing things the way they have always done them, and in tough economic times it is often difficult to buck the status quo and enter into new unknown areas. Compare the differing levels of success achieved by Borders and Amazon, HP and Apple, or Kodak and its digital counterparts.

As companies struggle to compete in a tight economy, it is more important than ever that they look to their most important resource—their people's wealth of knowledge and experience. When everyone in the organization is working toward the same goal, the perceived importance of competition between individuals, teams, and departments—which can lead to duplicated efforts, wasted resources, and lower productivity—is diminished. When material and intellectual assets are combined into one bucket from which the entire organization can draw, everyone can concentrate on coming up with innovative products, services, and operational improvements. The resulting success benefits all.

General Motors provides an example of how considerable time and money can be wasted when people in an organization do not collaborate. The company developed two in-house software drafting and manufacturing systems instead of having the body and mechanical divisions work together to develop one system that would work for both divisions. When they tried to merge the systems, they discovered that their lack of collaboration was going to be very expensive, not only because of the duplicated efforts but also because the two systems had to be integrated in order to function properly together. Keep in mind that the General Motors referred to here is essentially gone—that company went bankrupt, to be replaced by a newly created GM.

Collaboration with Competitors

Collaborating with "competitors" seems to be outside our comfort zone, an alien and self-defeating prospect. Why, we ask, should we help "them" beat us at our own game?

Increasingly, however, successful companies such as Toyota and Nissan are finding that by pooling their resources and competencies with their competitors, they can develop new innovative products and services and access new markets while significantly reducing costs. Although there are times when it is clearly worthwhile to defend company secrets, there are other areas where sharing knowledge with a select group will reduce costs or allow you to out-innovate every other competitor.

For one thing, strategic collaborations with selected competitors help companies avoid a serious problem inherent in the fiercely competitive economic theory that Americans consider "traditional": namely, reinventing the wheel or duplicating a basic method that has already been created or optimized by others. Many companies devote a great deal of money and energy to protecting proprietary resources such as trademarks, copyrights, and patents, when they could make better use of those resources by partnering with others to come up with mutually beneficial innovations. Of course, we aren't advocating sharing everything with everyone—you need to consider the situation carefully and calculate the likely negatives of sharing information and ideas versus the potential benefits. We are saying that although stamping "Confidential" on everything is easier than actually brainstorming possible alternatives, by being overly cautious you could miss out on valuable opportunities.

Instead of following the traditional model in which they would compete in an effort to become the first to produce electric cars, Tesla and Toyota are sharing their resources to achieve a mutually beneficial outcome: Toyota provides the plant and the vehicle manufacturing equipment, and Tesla provides the knowledge and expertise needed to produce its zero-emission premium electric sedan, the Model S. Tesla Motors and Toyota also signed an agreement to initiate the development of a second generation of the compact Toyota RAV4 EV that Toyota planned to introduce to the market by 2012. The RAV4 EV includes a lithium metal-oxide battery and other power train components supplied by Tesla (Ohnsman, 2010).

Nissan is another automobile company that realizes the importance of collaboration. In 2007, Minoru Shinohara, Nissan's general manager of the technology development division, said the company would not focus on designing hybrids but would instead concentrate on being able to start production of all-electric commuter cars, which they did with the 2011 rollout of the Nissan Leaf. The lithium polymer batteries for the cars are the result of a joint effort between Nissan and NEC. Nissan also has alliances with the major electric car service providers: Better Place, ECOtality, and eTec. The car maker's willingness to collaborate has resulted in a car that contributes to environmental sustainability and has greatly enhanced the sustainability of Nissan as a company (Kanellos, 2010).

Nissan has a long history of collaborations with several other companies. It has been able to stand out from the other automakers in this regard. For example, Nissan partnered with Ford for about a decade to sell its Mercury Villager and Nissan Quest minivans. These soon became popular in the United States, and Nissan was able to tap into Ford's expertise in the U.S. market.

Nissan also partnered with Austin, an established company in the UK, to gain access to the European markets. Nissan has collaborated with Austin for several years, producing and marketing Austins for many years and gaining the rights to use Austin patents that Nissan later used to develop high-quality engines.

Collaboration with Customers

One of the biggest changes seen in the emerging new economy is the development of more collaborative relationships with customers. Traditionally, customer relations have been viewed by many companies as "us against them." This adversarial stance was based on the idea that knowledge is power—and organizations were loath to share their power. But companies are now starting to see that when they view customers as partners and share knowledge with them, everyone benefits.

There are many ways in which companies can promote, solicit, implement, and reward collaboration and sharing throughout their supply chains. Encouraging ideas from suppliers can begin with standardized channels such as BMW's Virtual Innovation Agency (VIA), a web portal that supports supplier scouting, a forum for external innovators. Although the concept has been slow to take root at BMW, the idea has been inspirational. Many companies are now investing more resources in scouting out ideas in conjunction with suppliers through the use of web tools or events. In supplier innovation forums such as GM's three-day TechWorld conferences, suppliers and customers can discuss innovation trends and learn more about upcoming technological developments (Sloane, 2004).

Collaboration *and* Competition

Collaboration and competition are not mutually exclusive. It is important to stress that the most successful organizations are not collaborative all the time nor competitive all the time. The companies that realize the most success are those whose decisive leadership has thoughtfully considered when to collaborate and when to compete.

The fact is, there is no perfect method that can be applied to every situation. To paraphrase the psychologist Abraham Maslow, if the only tool you have is a hammer, it is tempting to treat everything as if it were a nail. Overreliance on the single familiar tool of competition is a problem that many organizations, especially those in the United States, struggle with. Sometimes, of course, the fiercely competitive hammer approach is the best way to achieve a goal; often, however, a more diplomatic, collaborative approach is the most effective and efficient way to get the job done. Competitors may need to hold back certain proprietary confidential concepts from the game, and they need to assess whether they can share enough relevant information and knowledge to make collaboration productive. In the same way that leaders need different styles for different situations, there is a time for hard-nosed competition and a time for more elaborately designed collaboration.

As evidence that neither competition nor collaboration is always right, compare the economic system of the United States with the economic system of Sweden. Americans and Swedes are both very innovative, yet they are very different in the way they approach the innovative process. Americans, who subscribe to Adam Smith's free-market economic theories, generally believe that competition is a main driver of innovation. The Swedes, on the other hand, are culturally rooted in their Jante Law, an unspoken code of ethics that embraces humility and rejects making oneself out as better than someone else. Their business community has an inclination to believe that collaboration and helping one's fellow citizen is the way to achieve great innovations that benefit oneself and society. Yet it is undeniable that both countries have made substantial contributions and that each has developed an impressive standard of living for its citizens. For example, both countries fall within the top ten in the Human Development Index (HDI), a comparative measure of life expectancy, literacy, education, and standards of living for countries worldwide.

The ability to select the best tool for a job and use that tool properly has a great deal to do with how easy the job is to accomplish and how successful the results are. Just as a plumber needs different tools to fix that leak under your sink and a computer technician needs different tools to be able to analyze and solve computer problems, executives and managers need more than one tool in their toolboxes to be able to use the one that's best in a given situation. Management speaker and business consultant Ken Blanchard, coauthor of *The One Minute Manager* and numerous other bestselling books, promotes a theory of situational leadership that is applicable here: true leaders remain flexible and open-minded. Good leaders recognize that there is nearly always more than one way to accomplish a goal and no single "best" style of leadership, and they use the right tool for the issue or people involved. In the same way, the successful organizations of the twenty-first century will be those that are most able to achieve a balance of competition and collaboration. In fact, an increasing number of organizations are doing just that.

One type of collaboration that lends itself nicely to a competitive-collaborative hybrid is the interfirm linkage. These operate under the notion that there are "three forms of accumulated capital—technical, commercial, and social," and rarely does one organization possess all three in an adequate quantity (Ahuja, 2000, p. 317). These shortages encourage a barter system wherein, for example, an organization with accumulated technical capital offers some of that capital in exchange for use of another organization's social capital. This type of collaboration can nestle itself nicely into a competitive market, perhaps adding the benefit of diversity and giving the collaboration an advantage over the remaining organizations that are standing alone. Good leaders recognize how to create the necessary balance.

Any of the many companies unfortunate enough to have been led by the notorious executive Al Dunlap felt the effect of this leader's having only one tool in his toolbox. In Dunlap's case the tool was a (figurative) chainsaw. He had only one management style—abrasive and destructive, featuring massive layoffs—and it earned him the nickname "Chainsaw Al." Dunlap was not interested in how to best handle situations for the good of the company. His one goal was to inflate a company's stock price, often artificially, to get the best price when he sold the company. He dealt with every situation in the same cutthroat manner, which forced many of the unfortunate companies under his command into bankruptcy.

Outsourcing as a Collaborative Venture

In the *Wall Street Journal*, Peter Drucker was quoted as advocating taking the portions of an organization that "do not make an absolute and quantifiable contribution to the bottom line" and paying someone else to do them (Drucker, 1989). Within the past two decades, a great many companies have done just that—and for good reason. Individual firms cannot be good at everything, and success in the new world depends on combining capabilities to get the job done as effectively and efficiently as possible. By subcontracting out various activities and aspects of producing their products and getting them to market, organizations are able to focus on their core competencies, streamline operations, increase efficiency, and improve both quality and customer service.

As companies are being forced to examine every possible area to eliminate as many excess costs as possible, it becomes increasingly important that they focus on what they do well and hand off extraneous tasks to individuals and organizations that specialize in that particular kind of work. The Human Capital Institute (HCI) reports that 90 percent of companies in the United States outsource some portion of the workload. According to the HCI survey, in 1990 only 6 percent of work done in the United States was performed by a worker who was not directly employed by the organization; by the early 2000s, that portion had increased to 27 percent (Lister, 2010).

As more and more organizations outsource, the practice becomes less and less of a competitive advantage and more of a necessity. But the only way for companies to fully leverage their outsourcing relationships and maximize the results is to embrace deep collaborative relationships with their outsourcing partners.

The quality of the collaboration realized in the relationship with the other company can ensure or impede the success of the outsourcing venture. In a research study conducted by CaseStack, participants who outsourced their transportation and logistics functions had an average 67 percent reduction in their carbon emissions. On-time performance for those participants was at least 98 percent, and they reported transportation cost reductions of up to 40 percent. Almost all also reported a reduction in their inventory, fewer damages, a reduced lead time, and a reduction in the amount of time their goods spent in transit. CaseStack attributes these results—which combined to maximize efficiency, lower shelf prices, decrease inventory costs, improve quality assurance, and garner a preferred status with their retailers—to the collaborative nature of the outsourcing relationship.

Outsourcing can also help reduce the amount of inventory carried and increase inventory velocity, providing companies with more expertise in peripheral areas and reducing the quantities of materials that need to be maintained in-house. An example of outsourcing inventory-related work is vendor-managed inventory (VMI), a collaborative process between a supplier or manufacturer and another manufacturer or a retailer or distributor, whereby the manufacturer gains access to the demand and inventory information at the retailer level and uses this information to directly manage the retailer's inventory. The VMI concept is one of the most widely used partnering initiatives for improving supply chain efficiency in the retail grocery industry today. First tested by Walmart and Procter & Gamble in the late 1980s, the pilot project led to lower inventory levels, fewer stockouts, and increased sales. Over time, successful VMI initiatives have been implemented by Johnson & Johnson, Frito Lay, Campbell Soup, the pasta manufacturer Barilla, and many other regional and national firms (Erkip, n.d.).

There are many other examples of companies using outsourcing to improve efficiency and thus compete more successfully. Apple designs the iPod in its Cupertino, California, offices, but it outsources the manufacturing to a few Chinese firms that not only build the product cheaply but also contribute unique intellectual property in materials science and packaging technology. In a manner of speaking, Apple also outsources content creation services to an open community of providers, from multibillion-dollar music publishers to amateur podcasters.

Although we tend to equate outsourcing with "offshoring," that is not always the case. Many companies are essentially "rural sourcing," "rural outsourcing," and "onshoring" within the United States or other developed countries. Although this is still outsourcing, the practice relies on the simple premise that some smaller towns offer a lower cost of living than urban centers, and some have people with very specialized skills, such as IT, accounting, retail, supply chain, and communication. Businesses that outsource work to these areas might expect to pay less than if they hired urbanites with comparable skills. Or they might find a unique set of skills uncommon in a larger city.

Numerous examples in the United States include towns with expertise in forest products in Maine and Oregon, financial services in South Dakota, automotive industries in Kentucky and South Carolina, medical devices in Colorado, multilingualism in Utah, and consumer packaged goods in Northwest Arkansas around Walmart's headquarters. As a result of Walmart's consumer packaged goods demand, this rural area has become home to more than 1,200 consumer packaged goods company locations. According to U.S. Census data that area now has the highest concentration of employment in the Management of Companies and Enterprises business sector compared to all MSAs nationwide.

There are many examples in the consumer goods industry in which outsourcing creates a powerful model. Apple & Eve, the largest independently owned juice company in the United States, outsources almost everything its company does. That's because the company's core function is to meet a need, not to make juice. The company started with the idea that people wanted healthier, more natural beverages, and their mission was to develop and sell a product that met that need. "[O]ur focus was to produce what our consumers wanted. We were not married to our production lines, because we didn't have any, so we outsourced all production. Not only did we outsource all production, but we outsourced all the growing and the pressing and bottling and transportation of the products, and therefore, it allowed us to focus on what we do best and that is, selling and marketing" (Landi, 2010). Successful outsourcing partners work at a very strategic level: redefining and broadened their understanding of "the organization" to include their full supply chains or collaborative networks. They increase their overall capabilities by sharing risks, rewards, and knowledge throughout their processes.

3

THE COLLABORATION PAYOFF

If everyone is moving forward together, then success takes care of itself.

—HENRY FORD

We can't do it alone. No one individual, no one civic organization, no well-meaning NGO, no single corporation can solve all of the many problems we face in this increasingly complex world. Just as "it takes a village" to raise a child, it takes the combined intelligence, skills, knowledge, and experience of groups of people working together toward a mutual goal to achieve new, innovative solutions to what have been called the "meta-problems" of today. Those collaborations take a lot of work. However, that work pays off in meaningful rewards to the collaborators and their organizations and to the world at large. For businesses, collaborative strategies can help increase sales, create innovative opportunities, improve customer service, and decrease costs. They can pave the way to new and better ways of operating.

There are examples from many aspects of life that help clarify why collaboration is well worth the effort. Increasingly, lifesaving medicines and medical procedures are developed, tested, approved, and made available through collaborative efforts. Collaborative projects are seeking ways to alleviate our climate and environmental problems. Artists are engaging in collaborations that result in both creative success and increased financial stability. Educational institutions collaborate with each other and with businesses, government, and philanthropic organizations to improve our schools and universities. Much of the technology that is changing our lives every day is based on collaborations.

We don't have to look far to find examples of collaborative efforts that are vitally important—even life-saving. Consider one collaboration that had enough star power that it sticks in most peoples' memories. Although a cynic might see it as nothing more than a song, many people remember the unique collaborative process that resulted in the hit single "We Are the World." In 1985, more than forty world-famous artists and musicians participated in the recording of the song, which is said to have sold more than twenty million copies worldwide and raised more than $63 million for humanitarian aid—an amazing demonstration of the way that the efforts of many people can be harnessed for good (USA for Africa, 2010).

Our world is even flatter today than it was in 1985, and we face an increasing number of seemingly intractable problems that ultimately affect us all: poverty, war, climate change, disease, and more. We're not going to solve these problems by continuing to do the same things we have been doing—otherwise they would have gone away by now. What we need to do is to find the innovative solutions that no one has thought of yet. To do that, we must harness our collective knowledge and talents through collaboration.

Most vital collaborative efforts don't involve the likes of Michael Jackson, Lionel Richie, Quincy Jones, and producer Michael Omartian, but those efforts are still saving and improving lives every day. A few examples:

- One of the biggest concerns in the hospital business is hospital-acquired infections (HAI), such as pneumonia, surgical site infections, and general cross-contamination. Even in a country like the United States, where hospitals are known for their hygiene and have highly trained health care workers, HAIs kill 100,000 people each year and affect 1.4 million people worldwide. HAIs have a significant impact on the U.S. health care system, creating an almost $7-billion annual impact with problems that include longer hospital stays, increased likelihood of readmission, and sizable added costs for patient care. In an effort to address this deadly problem, Kimberly-Clark Health Care created a collaborative health care professional education program called "Not on My Watch." Kimberly-Clark partnered with hospitals and other suppliers to work with doctors, designing and bringing accredited continuing education (CE) programs right to providers' facilities (Policy and Medicine, 2009). During a test at Emory University Hospital, the results were clear. Although some of the medical staff were initially skeptical, within three months after the project started, bloodstream infection rates were reduced from 3.6/1,000 patient days to 1/1,000 patient days. Reduced infections translates into lives saved. And Kimberly-Clark couldn't have done it alone. In addition to hospitals, doctors, and staffs, there are now over thirty-five organizations involved in the project, including the Centers for Disease Control (CDC), the U.S. Department of Defense, the World Health Organization (WHO), and a Kimberly-Clark competitor, Ortho-McNeil (HAI Watch).

• Clinovations Collaborative was started in November 2007 as a networking and learning collaborative in order to bring health care executives together to discuss pressing health care issues. The members are clinical and operational executives who are actively working at solving today's health care problems and providing insight with their relevant, real-world experience. These leaders have worked for the last two decades around the world to help advance improvements in health care, including patient safety and quality initiatives, hospital performance improvement, and electronic medical record implementation. Clinovations' collaborative goal is to provide its members, patients, health care providers, and others with access to leading practice information (Clinovations, n.d.).

• In 2004, UNESCO and the European Commission started supporting an initiative at National University of Rwanda to set up an independent radio station. Ever since the 1994 genocide in Rwanda, which
had been instigated by hate messages that were broadcast on the state-
dictated radio, this country's citizens had little trust in radio. There was
no plurality of sources and no variety. With the cooperation of UNESCO
and the European Commission, National University of Rwanda was able
to offer people an alternative news source, as well as an independent platform for discussion and debate (UNESCO, 2006).

• In April 2011, Missouri American Water teamed up with the U.S.
Drug Enforcement Administration (DEA) to encourage more than
150,000 households across Missouri to participate in the DEA's safe prescription drug disposal campaign. "Missouri American Water teams in
St. Louis County, St. Charles County, Mexico, Jefferson City, and
St. Joseph worked in collaboration with local law enforcement to promote
the program through a brochure included in local water bills. 'Historically,
unneeded medications have been flushed down the drain or thrown in the
trash. Prescription drug collection events give all of us an environmentally
responsible disposal method,' said Cindy Hebenstreit, Director of Water
Quality and Environmental Management" (Dettmer, 2011).

Not every collaboration is an obvious lifesaver, but each has a goal
that is important enough to bring people together. As mentioned by the
group that created this book's Foreword, it is unlikely that the U.S.
Constitution would be anything like it is now if it weren't for the intense
collaborative efforts of America's Founding Fathers. The Federalist Papers,
the Constitution, and the Declaration of Independence were all derived
through collaborative processes. These vital documents were not single-
handed works, but products of careful exchanges of worthy men who
were entrusted with responsibilities that were to define the course and the
history of what became the most powerful country in the world.

Collaborative undertakings, such as the drafting of those three documents, are an effective way to ensure that monopoly of both ideas and

styles is avoided. Furthermore, collaboration provides a checks-and-balances mechanism by providing opportunities for parties involved to challenge, seek clarification, verify, or even veto an idea or an action that goes against the overall vision and direction of the group. To appreciate the benefits that come with checks and balances, we need only to look at the conditions of societies ruled by dictators. Capturing diversity and maintaining the essence of representativeness in a social unit entails the often challenging but necessary collaboration among people with differing points of view.

Collaborate for Efficiency, Productivity, and Sustainable Innovation

Today's corporate leaders are charged with accomplishing more in less time and with fewer resources. Autonomous activities are being reevaluated and discarded as cumbersome, ineffective, inefficient, and costly. As mentioned in Chapter Two, a 2006 study by Frost & Sullivan, working with Microsoft and Verizon Business, found that collaboration is one of the key driving factors behind a company's performance (Microsoft, 2006).

The study indicated that its collaboration index, which was developed to include the two components of collaboration—capability and collaboration quality—has a greater positive impact on several important performance drivers within an organization than other factors. It had twice the positive effect of strategy orientation (pursuing new market opportunities) and five times that of market turbulence (the environment of the external market). The impact of the collaboration index showed that:

- Profitability increased 29 percent.
- Sales grew by 27 percent.
- Profit increased by 26 percent.
- Customer satisfaction increased by as much as 41 percent.
- Productivity increased by 36 percent.

- Product quality improved by 34 percent.
- Product development improved by 30 percent.
- Innovation grew 30 percent.

We generally see success coming from the companies that break from stereotypical, simple competition and opt for a more integrated collaborative approach. The leadership of those companies understands that economic, political, and technological environments change quickly and that an organization must be adaptable to keep up. To accomplish their goals, they must take steps to make their organizations more efficient and to achieve sustainable innovation by making high-level policy and structural changes that actively encourage, support, and reward both internal and external collaboration. The benefits are clear: organizations with a collaborative business model are able to create a larger market, offer better-quality products and services, and attain increased productivity, both now and in the future.

Business Benefits of Collaboration

Collaboration can create many advantages for a company, but the five benefits of collaboration most often mentioned are

- Leveraging R&D costs
- Positioning new ideas to create additional revenue through licensing or spin-off companies
- Redistribution and refocusing of resources
- Lower levels of risk with strategic experiments
- Development "from the outside in" (CPA Global, 2010)

Collaboration allows organizations to create greater leverage by increasing the ratio of output to effort. There is a lower level of risk when people collaborate because their combined knowledge and skills make it more likely that they will be able to handle all aspects of a task. Collaborating with others outside a closed group ("from the outside in") helps people come up with more innovative solutions than they could come up with on their own.

Let's look more closely at some specific ways in which collaboration pays off for organizations.

Increased Learning

Collaboration helps individuals and organizations learn and grow from the mutual sharing of knowledge, ideas, missions, and goals. Newer members learn from those with more experience, while the more experienced members benefit from the fresh perspectives and perhaps more current knowledge of the younger members. During a collaborative project, participants often explore and use new and unfamiliar resources and tools, which they can then draw on for future endeavors.

Improved, More Efficient R&D

Research and development is important for the survival of every company, but it need not be done in isolation. Today's market needs are so complex that it is beyond any one company to take responsibility for all R&D, even in a given niche. Effective collaboration can increase all the parties' chances of developing new and better products while saving them both time and money and eliminating duplicated effort that would result in similar technology.

The power of collaboration can be seen in the rapid advances being made in health care. Collaborations among people from health care, biotech companies, government, and universities are bearing fruit in terms of new ways to diagnose disease and test new drugs. Twenty-three years ago there was only one treatment option for people with HIV. Today, collaborations within the scientific community have resulted in more than thirty-three antiretroviral drugs that have been approved for treatment, with several more in clinical trials. There are now five medicines available for Alzheimer's patients, with many more under development. To "leverage internal innovations with external expertise," Abbott Laboratories has created an Advanced Technology team that "scours the globe in search of potential new partnerships with those in academia, government, biotechnology and other industries." A collaborative partnership between Eli Lilly and Medtronic brings the expertise of both companies together in the attempt to develop a new, more effective approach to treating Parkinson's disease (Eli Lilly and Company, 2011). The list goes on.

Increased Innovation

One of the most valuable outcomes of collaborative projects is the true innovation that happens when people with a diversity of experience, knowledge, and perspectives work together to achieve a common goal. Although collaboration often entails the challenging management of differing ideas, clashing personalities, unyielding members, conflict, friction, and opposition that inevitably comes with bringing together people who have different ways of doing things, the results can be well worth the effort. One person, one organization, or an isolated group of people with similar knowledge and perspectives is less likely to come up with truly innovative solutions or new ways of doing things, because they tend to see things from the same point of view.

In fact, true innovation—the creation of something that no one has thought of before—can result when large numbers of people from different industries, organizations, and cultures put their minds to solving the same problem. For example, in 1943, a GE engineer was trying to create a low-cost rubber substitute that would help with the war effort. The resulting product was a failure as a rubber substitute. Still, GE continued to send the formula to various engineers around the world, looking for a way to put the substance to practical use. They never did find a *practical* use, but this open innovation led to what turned out to be a very popular product: Silly Putty (Moore, 2010). Open innovation frequently leads to discoveries of this kind that make a marketplace buzz with activity.

Another notable innovation example can be seen at GreenXchange, a collaboration platform that was started by Creative Commons in collaboration with Nike and Best Buy. A digital system launched in early 2010, GreenXchange promotes open innovation and provides a place where companies can share and adopt technologies related to sustainability issues. The platform provides a set of free standardized legal tools that patent owners can use to make their technology available to others, with the option of receiving annual licensing payments. The ten early collaborators—Best Buy, Creative Commons, IDEO, Mountain Equipment Co-op, Nike, nGenera (now Moxie Software), Outdoor Industry Association, salesforce.com, 2degrees, and Yahoo!—encouraged others, including academic researchers, to join them in committing their intellectual property for everyone's benefit. Their collaborative efforts focus the best minds on working together to solve our toughest sustainability problems.

This kind of open innovation benefits both the organizations themselves and the larger world that we all share. It helps companies reduce the costs of innovation by making it unnecessary to duplicate research on ways to reduce the environmental impact of their products and operations. It also gives smaller companies access to the knowledge they need to establish energy-efficient operations and sustainable business practices.

According to John Wilbanks, VP of science at Creative Commons, the GreenXchange platform makes it simpler, faster, and more cost-effective for organizations to share their intellectual property. "There is so much duplication of effort and wasted resources when it comes to sustainability," Wilbanks says, that "we need to make it easier for individuals, companies, academia, and researchers to collaborate and share best practices in order to create and adopt technologies that have the potential to solve global sustainability challenges" (Nike, 2010).

When making intellectual property available through GreenXchange, companies can choose the licensing approach they prefer. One GreenXchange in-person "collaboratory" brought together a typically adversarial group that included Brooks, Nike, New Balance, and the Environmental Protection Agency to discuss packaging issues. Each will still compete in many ways, but they had common interests such as running shoe recycling, water-based adhesives, "green leather," and energy efficiency at manufacturing plants (Nike, 2010).

Access to a Larger Resource Pool

One of the key benefits of collaboration is that it allows organizations to make the best use of their resources, including their human capital, technical know-how, materials, tools, and online utilities. This can be extremely helpful for large businesses, which can collaborate with local businesses to better focus on small projects, as well as for smaller organizations that may not have all the resources they need to accomplish all their goals.

In a typical situation, a small business collaborates with a large firm to enter a highly competitive global market that the large firm has dominated. The small company has the knowledge, skills, and technology to develop a specific product but lacks essential resources to bring it to market, such as credibility, marketing capability, a distribution network, and funding. The large company, on the other hand, lacks the flexibility and innovative capacity to respond quickly to changing customer requirements. In that situation, collaboration can benefit both companies, helping them reduce risk while achieving higher sales and profits. The large company is able to maintain its position as market leader, and the small company can realize its potential (McNabb & O'Neill, 1996).

Reduced Need to Reinvent the Wheel

By helping to prevent the replication of services, collaboration lets companies stay lean so they can compete effectively in the market. Strategic alliances allow firms to focus on their competencies by teaming up with companies that have complementary resources. In many circumstances, going it alone would not make economic sense; by partnering and sharing the financial rewards, everyone involved in the collaboration ends up profiting. For example, when companies open up their technologies for use by other companies, as Toyota did with the hybrid engine it developed for the Prius, those other companies are relieved of the time and expense of discovering the same solutions on their own. They can simply use existing technologies that have been shown to be effective, thus saving valuable resources that can be used in other ways.

In a partnership described by Mark Kaufman in the *Washington Post*, NASA and Google collaborated to make NASA's vast store of images from space missions available to the public. According to Chris C. Kemp, director of strategic business development at NASA, "NASA has collected and processed more information about our planet and universe than any other entity in the history of humanity. . . . Even though this information was collected for the benefit of everyone, and much is in the public domain, the vast majority of this information is scattered and difficult for non-experts to access and to understand." Kemp went on to explain that Google and NASA were "bringing together some of the best research scientists and engineers." NASA provides weather forecasting information, three-dimensional maps of the moon and Mars, and real-time tracking of the International Space Station and Space Shuttle flights; Google provides some financial support for agency projects and uses NASA images on its Google Earth website (Kaufman, 2006).

Large Projects Handled More Easily

Large companies often face very complicated problems involving multiple locations, people, systems, and outside companies that stand in the way of big payoffs. Collaboration allows projects that are too large or complex for one group to handle to be spanned across different departments, teams, or organizations. Being able to bring people together to collaborate on a solution can deliver results. For example, Nucor is the largest producer of steel in the United States and the world's leading steel recycler. In mid-2010, after a devastating flood in Nebraska in an area that was home to four Nucor divisions, the company was able to get up and running again quickly because they created a large-scale collaborative project that included sister companies, customers, vendors, and local and federal governments. Working in collaboration with one another, making sure that each party knew what all the other parties were doing and that all were holding each other accountable, the members of the team brought together a massive construction process and shifts in technology and operational strategies, so that permits could be granted, shipping hours could be increased, and local road and rail infrastructure could be prioritized (Griffith, 2010).

An even bigger example is the recent collaboration between China and the United States. In January 2011, China's President Hu Jintao visited the United States to meet with President Barack Obama. The leaders reaffirmed their commitment to building a positive relationship between the countries. They agreed that broader and deeper collaboration with international partners is required to develop and implement sustainable solutions and to promote peace, stability, prosperity, and the well-being of global society.

The presidents recognized the importance of the world's two largest economies' working together to build a cooperative economic partnership to benefit both countries as well as the global economy. They agreed that a framework should be developed to further allow for economic cooperation.

The two countries' collaboration efforts are demonstrating substantial results. In the U.S.-China Strategic and Economic Dialogue (S&ED) they produced twenty-six specific outcomes on topics including nuclear safety, environmental sustainability, supply chain security, and maritime rescue cooperation. As result of these initiatives, it is expected that food supply chains will become safer, illegal trafficking of nuclear materials will be prevented, and pollution will be reduced (U.S. Department of State, 2010).

Exploration of New Markets

Collaboration offers companies the opportunity to explore new markets to which they might otherwise not have access. An example: in February 2011, an Ernst and Young news release announced that pharmaceutical companies are "increasing their investments in new and innovative offerings to meet the demands of a patient-empowered, data-driven, outcomes-focused future in health care." In 2010, investments by pharmaceutical companies in smart phone apps, educational websites, social media platforms, wireless devices, and other programs increased 78 percent. According to the news release, "many of these initiatives involve collaborating in new ways with non-pharmaceutical companies."

The news release quotes Ernst & Young Life Sciences Leader Patrick Flochel, EMEIA: "Success in Pharma 3.0 will require diverse capabilities—from the ability to mine insights from vast pools of dissimilar health data, to rural distribution networks in emerging markets and wireless communication platforms . . . No single company has everything that it will take. And in today's resource-strapped business climate, companies will benefit by leveraging investments that other companies have already made, rather than reinventing every wheel. Collaboration—radical collaboration, and lots of it—is the future" (Tanna & Kelley, 2011).

Time Savings

Another major advantage of collaboration is the significant amount of potential time savings. Effective collaboration is a critical component of product development that can deliver significant time saving value across an organization. If the design, engineering, manufacturing, sales, and marketing groups are able to collaborate in real time when managing changes, all groups can quickly work to agreeable solutions, saving time, effort, and rework. When all stakeholders in the product development process have instant access to the most current product definition data and models, manufacturers can achieve a number of desired benefits. Collaborative efforts can reduce time-to-market at some of the most critical junctures for many innovative companies. In addition, the process lowers overall product development costs. After all, time is money; with secure web-based sharing and storage of data, companies can not only reduce travel expenses associated with product development activities but also lower administration costs when generating and disseminating information. Plus, by reducing the number of errors generated, companies save money on fewer change requests, reduced scrap, and less rework.

Trade Promotion Collaboration Saves Time

Of the retailers surveyed by DemandTec and Booz Allen Hamilton, "92 percent said collaboration was 'very important' and 8 percent, 'important.' Of the manufacturers, 56 percent rated collaboration 'very important' and

39 percent, 'important.' Key benefits of collaboration cited by both sides include not only ROI and effective promotions, but also revenue growth and more efficient planning" (Ryan, 2007). Collaboration saved time that would have been spent planning, while improving returns.

In an April 2011 press release, Ahold USA, which operates nearly three thousand supermarkets across the United States and Europe, reported that a collaboration with their manufacturing trading partners on the DemandTec End-to-End Promotion Management resulted in significant time and cost savings by eliminating the need for labor-intensive manual data entry. According to DemandTec, the system was used to link the trading partners and enable them to:

- Effectively plan, negotiate, execute, and track win-win promotions;

- Improve promotion effectiveness, with the ability to forecast the impact of promotions and tactics using proven analytics;

- Deliver more targeted and localized messages to customers by automating promotion versions; and

- Efficiently access a single system of record for promotions and events. (Retail Touch Points, 2011)

"'In the dynamic retail industry, competition has become increasingly fierce, and the ability to efficiently and effectively manage promotions is a competitive advantage,' said Kevin Sterneckert, Research Director for Consumer Value Chain at Gartner, Inc. 'Successful retailers are moving closer to managing this complex process in an integrated and collaborative manner from end-to-end with their trading partners'" (Retail Touch Points, 2011).

Improved Training

Although training is an essential cost for most organizations, many organizations are not able to provide the most complete, up-to-the-moment training on their own. By pooling their resources, collaborative partners can provide better training facilities and increased opportunities to each other's staff members while lowering their training costs.

For example, the Disney Institute, the professional development and external training arm of the Walt Disney Company, offers programs for professionals from many different industries, including health care, aerospace/aviation, government/military, food/beverage, and retail. The Disney Institute was formerly a resort and learning center, opened in February 1996 by Michael Eisner. Partly based on the Chautauqua Institution in New York, it was envisioned as a new direction in vacationing: more about hands-on learning, personal development, and interactivity rather than the passive, entertainment-based experience traditionally offered in Disney's theme parks. Although the original facility has been closed, the content is still served up at different locations (hotels and universities), and Disney Institute instructors have compiled their customer service courses in a book titled *Be Our Guest: Perfecting the Art of Customer Service.*

Many community colleges and universities throughout the country are now working more closely with companies to ensure that their courses adequately prepare graduates to enter the workforce. One such institution is Northeastern University in Boston, which integrates rigorous classroom studies with experiential learning opportunities, anchored by the nation's largest, most innovative cooperative education program. Through this program, students can gain up to eighteen months of paid professional experience—experience that is integrated with their studies, stimulating them to connect ideas with action. They build a résumé, sample careers that match their interests and abilities, meet potential employers, develop valuable job-search and interviewing skills, and gain self-confidence through professional achievement. Colleges and universities throughout the country also work closely with local businesses to provide technical and professional development courses for their employees.

Collaboration for Sustainability

As mentioned earlier, given the importance of business-environmental sustainability and its connection to collaboration, it merits a closer look. This is especially true because our new capacity to collaborate is fundamental to empowering the sustainability paradigm shift. Many business people have already embraced the concept that sustainability will be a key driver of business success in the coming decades, but few realize that its underpinnings are primarily driven by the world's new capabilities relating to collaboration. In a 2008 issue of the *Journal of Management*, Sebastian Raisch and Julian Birkinshaw described the concept of "organizational ambidexterity." In academic circles, organizational ambidexterity refers to an entity's ability to be efficient in their management of today's business and also adaptable for coping with tomorrow's changing demands. In practical terms, collaborative organizations and networks usually develop considerable organizational ambidexterity because of the fluidity that comes with diverse knowledgeable professionals working so closely together (Raisch & Birkinshaw, 2008). The successful application of sustainable business practices requires that an organization be able to use collaboration and the resulting organizational ambidexterity to break down silos. The game-changing wins come from cross-company, cross-function, and cross-organization collaborations.

Business-environmental sustainability is still often misconstrued as a revival of the green movement of the 1960s, but nothing could be further from the truth. This new business sustainability trend has far more potential than the original green movement, primarily because collaborative principles are making organizational sustainability more feasible. And although billions of people in developing countries are starting to behave more like their developed country counterparts, there won't be enough resources for seven to nine billion people to continue voraciously using resources without some big changes. We will need technology to help make both human survival and business profitability possible in the face of scarcity. In this case, though, the technology must support sustainability, and its foundation is collaboration.

The earlier green movement focused largely on environmental awareness and reducing our resource consumption. Although sustainability does include a civic environmental benefit, it goes well beyond that to encompass the economic incentives of waste reduction as well. Delivering on these issues almost always requires multiple parties to come together in collaboration to succeed.

Leaders of organizations who expect their companies to endure have begun thinking beyond the short term toward more long-term plans that consider the likelihood of dramatic changes in resource availability. This concept is sometimes called the "triple bottom line," a phrase coined by John Elkington in his 1998 book *Cannibals with Forks: The Triple Bottom Line of 21st Century Business.* The "three pillars" of the triple bottom line are people, planet, and profit.

People refers to business practices that are fair in terms of the workforce and the community; a sustainable business seeks to benefit people, not exploit or endanger them. Thus a business might choose to sell only fair trade products, refuse to deal with companies that use child labor, ensure that all its employees have access to good health care, and find ways to give back to the community by supporting schools.

Planet refers to business practices that help to protect the environment and save natural resources. That means taking steps to reduce the use of energy, recycle, and render waste nontoxic and dispose of it carefully so it does not add to pollution. A business concerned about the planet might reduce the amount of packaging it uses, treat waste before releasing it into the atmosphere or the river, use recycled materials when possible, and install LED light bulbs and solar panels. It might provide funds and technical expertise to help its community build parks, clean up polluted streams, and educate people on ways to save energy.

Profit, without which a business cannot survive and grow, "is the economic value created by the organization after deducting the cost of all inputs, including the cost of the capital tied up. . . . Within a sustainability framework, the 'profit' aspect needs to be seen as the real economic benefit enjoyed by the host society. . . . the real economic impact the organization has on its economic environment" (Elkington, 1998).

Unilever offers an example of the relationship between this concept and business success. Under conventional notions of how to run a conglomerate like Unilever, CEO Patrick Cescau should wake up each morning with a laser-like focus: how to sell more soap and shampoo than Procter & Gamble. But ask Cescau about the $52 billion Dutch-British giant's biggest strategic challenges for the twenty-first century, and the conversation roams from water-deprived villages in Africa to the planet's warming climate.

In Brazil, Unilever operates a free community laundry in a São Paulo slum, provides financing to help tomato growers convert to eco-friendly drip irrigation, and recycles seventeen tons of waste annually at a toothpaste factory. The company funds a floating hospital that offers free medical care in Bangladesh, a nation with just twenty doctors for every ten thousand people. In Ghana, Unilever teaches palm oil producers to reuse plant waste while providing potable water to deprived communities. In India, Unilever's staff helps thousands of women in remote villages start micro-enterprises. The company discloses how much carbon dioxide and hazardous waste its factories spew out around the world.

As Cescau sees it, helping such nations wrestle with poverty, water scarcity, and the effects of climate change is vital to staying competitive in coming decades. Some 40 percent of the company's sales and most of its growth now take place in developing nations. Unilever food products account for roughly 10 percent of the world's crops of tea and 30 percent of all spinach. It is also one of the world's biggest buyers of fish. As environmental regulations grow tighter around the world, Unilever must invest in green technologies or its leadership in packaged foods, soaps, and other goods could be imperiled. "You can't ignore the impact your company has on the community and environment," Cescau says. CEOs used to frame thoughts like these in the context of moral responsibility, he adds. But now, "it's also about growth and innovation. In the future, it will be the only way to do business."

A remarkable number of CEOs have begun to commit themselves to the same kind of sustainability goals. For years, the term "sustainability" has carried a lot of baggage. But it's really about meeting humanity's needs without harming future generations. It's long been a favorite cause among economic development experts, human rights activists, and conservationists, but to many U.S. business leaders, sustainability just meant higher costs and smacked of earnest U.N. corporate-responsibility conferences and the utopian idealism of Western Europe. Today, however, sustainability is "right at the top of the agendas" of an increasing number of U.S. CEOs, especially those who have recently entered leadership roles, says McKinsey Global Institute Chairman Lenny Mendonca.

Embracing sustainability can help companies avert costly setbacks from environmental disasters, political protests, and human rights or workplace abuses—the kinds of debacles suffered by Royal Dutch Shell PLC (RDS) in Nigeria and Unocal in Burma. "Nobody has an idea when such events can hit a balance sheet, so companies must stay ahead of the curve," says Matthew J. Kiernan, CEO of Innovest Strategic Value Advisors, an international research and advisory firm that prepared a list of the world's one hundred most sustainable corporations. The roster includes Jeffrey Immelt, CEO of GE, who is betting billions to position GE as a leading innovator in everything from wind power to hybrid engines; Walmart, which has made a series of high-profile promises to slash energy use overall; GlaxoSmithKline (GSK), which discovered that, by investing to develop drugs for poor nations, it can work more effectively with those governments to make sure its patents are protected; and Dow Chemical Company, which is increasing R&D in products such as roof tiles that deliver solar power to buildings and water treatment technologies for regions short of clean water. "There is 100 percent overlap between our business drivers and social and environmental interests," says Dow CEO Andrew N. Liveris.

Striking that balance is not easy. Many noble efforts fail because they are poorly executed or never made sense to begin with. Harvard University business guru Michael Porter, speaking of sustainability, says, "If there's no connection to a company's business, it doesn't have much leverage to make an impact." It can be a hard proposition for investors, too. Decades of experience show that it's risky to pick stocks based mainly on a company's long-term environmental or social-responsibility targets.

Nevertheless, new sets of metrics, which Innovest and others designed to measure sustainability efforts, have helped convince CEOs and boards that those efforts pay off.

Rising investor demand for information on sustainability has spurred a flood of new research. Goldman Sachs, Deutsche Bank Securities, Union Bank of Switzerland (UBS), Citigroup, Morgan Stanley, and other brokerages have formed dedicated teams assessing how companies are affected by everything from climate change and social pressures in emerging markets to governance records. "The difference in interest between three years ago and now is extraordinary," says former Goldman Sachs Asset Management CEO David Blood, who heads the Enhanced Analytics Initiative—a research effort on intangibles conducted by twenty-two brokerages—as well as Generation Investment Management, cofounded in 2004 with former Vice President Al Gore, which uses sustainability as an investment criterion.

Perhaps the most ambitious effort is by Innovest, founded in 1995 by Kiernan, a former KPMG senior partner. Besides conventional financial performance metrics, Innovest studies 120 different factors, such as energy use, health and safety records, litigation, employee practices, regulatory history, and management systems for dealing with supplier problems. It uses these measures to assign grades ranging from AAA to CCC, much like a bond rating, to 2,200 listed companies that excel at tailoring products for developing nations and banks that study the environmental impact of projects they help finance.

What makes progress on sustainability powerful and even possible is that businesses are now willing and able to collaborate. Several competitive companies in today's marketplace have used the methods of collaboration to stand apart from the crowd. The ability of these companies to change in response to newer demands has helped them emerge as winners, even in tough times. These companies create a sustainable environment in the workplace; indeed, their whole business model is based on sustainability.

As a poster child for the concept of redesigning a business to meet the demands and opportunities of the twenty-first century, one need look no further than the largest company in the world—Walmart. Lee Scott, the former CEO, began exploring sustainability back in the mid-2000s because

Walmart had a negative reputation, particularly in metro areas where it had few stores and wanted to open more. The sustainability message originally seemed like a good marketing strategy for improving Walmart's relationships with new potential customers. But in 2005, Scott began what he has described as a journey to see sustainability as something bigger—something essential to Walmart's long-term viability. The company's leadership came to see pollution as synonymous with waste, and there's nothing more taboo in Walmart's culture than waste. Waste costs money that could be used to lower prices; lower prices drive more business; thus waste is bad. A cleaner, greener, more efficient Walmart, the leadership realized, would be able to deliver lower prices to customers and more profits to shareholders.

With that realization in mind, Walmart's leadership embarked on an aggressive initiative that continues to change the consumer packaged goods industry today. Packages for toys became smaller, laundry detergents were concentrated, auxiliary power units were installed on company trucks, and LED lights and greener refrigerants were rolled out into the warehouses and stores. Their goals are impressive:

- To be supplied 100 percent by renewable energy
- To create zero waste
- To sell products that sustain people and the environment

Achieving these goals depends on full participatory collaboration with many of the about sixty thousand suppliers who provide goods and services to Walmart. Like any collaboration-based initiative, it has costs and benefits for all participants. General Mills is one example of how sweeping the changes are. General Mills went as far as straightening out its Hamburger Helper noodles, so the product could lie flatter in the box, which allows General Mills to reduce the size of those boxes. The move saved nearly 900,000 pounds of paper fiber every year and it reduced the company's greenhouse gas emissions by 11 percent by taking 500 trucks off the road. It also increased the number of Hamburger Helper boxes on Walmart shelves by 20 percent. That change was more than a win-win—it increased profits at both General Mills and Walmart, and it also benefited Walmart shoppers. Thousands of similar modifications led by Walmart's initiative allow shoppers to truly save money, so their families can live better.

In 2009, Walmart provided initial funding for a sustainability consortium composed of universities that are collaborating with suppliers, retailers, nongovernmental organizations, and government officials to develop a system for rating electronics based on their level of environmental and social responsibility and educate customers and industries about their impact on the environment and society. The consortium, which is administered by Arizona State University and the University of Arkansas, has been able to attract leading companies such as Dell, HP, Intel, and Toshiba that have defined what it means to go green in the electronics industry (The Sustainability Consortium, n.d.).

As with any new innovation, there are always unknowns and risks that need to be identified and managed. One reason distinct collaborative groups can be powerful is that they often work outside the normal box at an organization. If you think about most people in an organization, they are trying to move their careers forward. As a result, they tend to focus on marginal, evolutionary ideas. A separate collaborative team can open their eyes to larger revolutionary ideas. Charles Leadbeater touched on this in a TEDGlobal talk in July 2005: "Do you go in to your board and say, look, I've got a fantastic idea for an embryonic product in a marginal market, with consumers we've never dealt with before, and I'm not sure it's going to have a big payoff, but it could be really, really big in the future? No, what you do, is you go in and you say, I've got a fantastic idea for an incremental innovation to an existing product we sell through existing channels to existing users, and I can guarantee you get this much return out of it over the next three years" (Leadbeater, 2005). The normal hierarchical structure makes it difficult to advance really big ideas; a collaborative team, on the other hand, may not be hindered to think about new, bigger ideas. There are endless examples of the payoffs from collaboration, but each requires leadership to cast off traditional methods to try something new and unknown.

4

RISKS OF COLLABORATION

*In order to succeed, your desire for success should be
greater than your fear of failure.*

—BILL COSBY

There is a time and a place to use collaborative business practices.
Used in incorrect circumstances, collaboration can be unsuccessful,
counterproductive, or even risky. However, many problems can be
avoided or mitigated with planning and the recognition of potential risks.
Some of the most obvious and most important risks that must be
addressed and managed in a collaborative setting are data security, intellectual property, legal and antitrust issues, and reputational risks.

Data Security

The collaboration tools that allow quick and convenient information
sharing between the parties also make it essential for IT departments to
use safeguards and establish best practices to ensure data security within

their organizations. File encryption and user authentication are essential elements of making sure that data is secure yet accessible to the collaborators. In addition to IT-based data safeguards, you must establish strong governance, including policies and guidelines for use, and provide resources to help participants choose appropriate tech or service solutions. Make sure the platforms are appropriately sized and ensure that they are moderated and monitored. Realizing that each team member might be at a different technology level, it is important to make sure that collaboration tools are easy for everyone to use. Whether people admit to a need or not, make training resources readily available. Each tool learned for the project will likely pay off in spades for many of the participants.

Intellectual Property

Give intellectual property a lot of thought. If you have valuable IP, it is worth careful analysis and double-checking a few times to make sure the IP issue can be managed. The potential for IP theft or misappropriation is a very real risk, so deep consideration is needed when deciding whether to collaborate with a potential partner. The World Customs Organization estimated that IP theft was responsible for worldwide lost sales of $500–$600 billion yearly (Schmitz, 2011). Making sure that any necessary legal documents are in place will not only protect collaborators but also give them the sense of security and freedom to fully engage in the collaboration. It is important to define the appropriate use of intellectual property by the participants. Define a clear purpose and boundaries and create a code of conduct. If information posting is involved, ensure that there is a paper trail; allow no anonymity. Although we all enjoy the convenience of email, there is no way to tell whether others have started reviewing a document or have even opened it, so use tools to manage that where necessary. As part of the code of conduct, establish appropriate moderation, define etiquette, and establish something of a social contract for participants. Depending on the level of shared intellectual property, it may be important to differentiate between "inward-facing" and "out-ward-facing" information, balancing access based on needs and risks.

Frankly, there are times when the risks inherent in the information sharing requirements will make collaboration prohibitive. Recently Congress has considered whether the White House Office of Science and Technology Policy (OSTP) and the National Aeronautics and Space Administration (NASA) should limit some types of collaboration with some international trading partners. Some U.S. congressional representatives believe that collaboration will allow foreign companies to take advantage of U.S. technology, and that the United States has little to gain from sharing. There have been mentions of potential spying, cyber-attacks, and technology theft from U.S. companies. In the past few years, we have seen claims of hacking into computers that contain foreign policy and human rights information. The American global aerospace and defense technology company Northrop Grumman has created a chronology of alleged foreign cyber-espionage incidents targeting U.S. and foreign governments. Although these relate to big government and corporate issues, the concepts translate to any intercompany and even intracompany sharing.

Sharing is important, but knowledge is power, and the data it is derived from must be controlled. When dealing with document management, also consider these seemingly mundane topics: rights and version control. Throughout the process, each document should always have a responsible document owner; the person with all of the rights. The owner will be responsible for managing the document and guaranteeing that it gets where it needs to go in a timely fashion. That same individual or group can coordinate and calibrate input from different authors to smooth out any issues that may arise. And you cannot assume that everyone uses the same version control techniques—or, for that matter, that they even know what it means. Use readily available "track changes" functionality and agreed-upon, standardized file naming conventions. If each party uses his own favorite file naming convention, you will invariably end up with versions getting lost in the shuffle. It is tremendously frustrating to lose work due to poor version control—and it's avoidable, with a good system in place.

Legal and Antitrust Issues

There's a flip side to collaboration that can result in important legal antitrust risks. We have laws, rules, regulations, and cultures within which businesses must operate. Breaching these boundaries can lead to undesirable consequences, some of which can be very serious. Even a collaborative venture that appears to be highly positive and ethical might cross the line into illegality, transgressing the anticompetition and antitrust laws that are designed to protect consumers by keeping prices down and quality up.

Both collaborative practices and collusive practices such as price fixing, market division, and bid rigging involve rival companies working together in a cooperative manner. The difference is one of intent: although collusion may be beneficial to the organizations involved, it is seldom in the best interest of their customers. Collaboration, on the other hand, is undertaken as a way to benefit both the participating companies and their customers. It is in the best interest of participants to obey an even higher standard than the law of the land—to try to avoid even the appearance of impropriety. With that level of conscientiousness in mind, it is likely the collaborating organizations can steer very clear of any worst-case legal implications.

It is only right that companies that end up breaking the law are dealt with severely; they have violated a very basic principle of our capitalist economy and caused harm to consumers and the system. For example, in 1960, in the first related case to send corporate executives to prison, federal indictments were handed down to more than fifty executives at General Electric, Westinghouse, and several other electrical equipment makers for violating the price-fixing ban of the Sherman Antitrust Act of 1890. The companies' collusion to fix prices of heavy equipment sold to government agencies went on for decades and is estimated to have cost taxpayers $175 million for each year they were engaged in the practice.

In 1996, Archer Daniels Midland (ADM) was given the largest price-fixing fine ever, $100 million, for fixing prices of two products: lysine, which is used in livestock feed, and citric acid, which is used in detergent and soft drinks. By agreeing with competitors to illegally inflate prices, the company overcharged its customers and did not allow the market to work correctly.

Keep in mind that these instances are very unusual. Although it is worthwhile to understand risks and boundaries, realize that businesses do themselves and their customers a disservice by avoiding all collaboration; it is perfectly legal and beneficial for consumers. It is virtually impossible for companies to accidentally fix prices. But be aware of the risks of simply assuming that all laws are being followed by all collaborators; make sure there will not be even an appearance of improper or illegal actions. The objective is to help consumers!

Reputational Risks

We have all heard the saying, "You are known by the company you keep." Businesses, like individuals, must ensure that their associations are not with any person or entity of questionable character. Even if actual practices do not rise to the level of being illegal, there may be dubious activities that are best avoided. Before entering into any relationships, it is important to know the character of your potential partners. With the current widespread access to information, it is becoming impossible to hide character flaws. Do the research, and if you find one questionable issue, don't give it the benefit of the doubt. If someone has taken a hiatus from good behavior once, they will do it again. Your reputation is at risk.

In addition to the specific risks that may be encountered, there are a number of other situations that simply may not be appropriate for collaboration. When people try to collaborate at the wrong time, in the wrong place, and in the wrong way, it is not only frustrating and wasteful, it is counterproductive and perhaps even harmful.

Collaboration does require an investment in time and resources. Although collaboration can make many projects more productive, it increases efficiency only when used in the right situation, with the right people, for the right reasons, and with the full support of the people who have the authority to implement the results. It's important to keep in mind that the point of collaboration is to maximize the use of resources, especially human capital, and create an outcome far greater than the sum of all the parts.

Some organizations will likely have a more natural inclination toward innovation and collaboration. One would expect younger, startup companies with entrepreneurial cultures to have some advantages in this department. Collaboration will likely be more easily accomplished, and therefore less risky, with nimble smaller companies. This should not be taken to imply that collaborating with larger, established organizations may be too challenging to be worthwhile. Keep in mind that the largest opportunities often lie behind the walls of the largest organizations. All organizations—big and small—need to be scalable to be worthwhile, and an organization of any size can retain its innovative culture. But to reduce the risk of fruitless efforts, it is important to penetrate any organization before rushing into a collaborative relationship—understand the culture. Small or large, if the organization can't make decisions without endless obstacles, collaboration efforts may prove hollow. Every organization's leadership thinks they are innovative, but innovation is just a word if it isn't actually respected, invested in, and practiced.

There are other situations that present a risk of failure. Collaboration is likely to be unsuccessful, a waste of time and resources, and even detrimental in the following types of situations:

- There are tight time constraints.

- The project isn't important enough to be worth the effort.

- The result is unlikely to significantly improve the situation or achieve something worthwhile.

- The group lacks the authority or support needed to implement the results.

- The group lacks sufficient diversity.
- The reasons for participation are misaligned.
- Bad things happen when bad guys collaborate.

Let's look more closely at each of these situations.

Tight Time Constraints

Successful collaborations take time: to identify and assemble a group, provide people with the skills they need to collaborate effectively, define and clarify goals, agree on communication and decision-making methods, gather information, generate ideas, and develop implementation plans. Rushing the process or attempting to complete a collaborative project with a group that is new to collaborating can be a recipe for failure. After collaborative skills are mastered, they can stimulate innovation and result in efficiencies that save significant amounts of time. But if a project has a limited time frame and the participants are not accustomed to collaborating, the effort may well end up a disappointment and thus a waste of everyone's time.

We see some of the negative effects of time constraints on collaboration when we look at government mandates that require companies and industries to collaborate with one another, yet set unrealistic deadlines. Too often, everyone involved becomes frustrated and the goal is not accomplished. One example is the deadlines set by the American Recovery and Reinvestment Act (ARRA) of 2009, which didn't give tech companies enough time to work together, so that money invested appears to have had low returns.

Emergency situations can demonstrate that collaboration is not always best. Sometimes, following a clear-cut, established hierarchy is the most efficient way to approach a problem (Erickson, 2010). For example, hospital emergency room staff members each have a well-defined role to play. Regardless of which nurse is working with which doctor, their role in the group determines which task they will perform. They do not trade tasks, and they do not have time to reach group consensus. They follow a clear hierarchy to make sure that each needed function will be carried out as efficiently as possible. If the same group of medical care providers were assembled in a group with no specified roles, valuable time would be wasted as each group member jockeyed for position. In an emergency situation, it is best to follow the established, clearly defined and assigned job functions and cooperate rather than attempt to collaborate. If you were seriously injured, would you want to check into an emergency room where roles are pre-set or one where the staff will be using time to collaborate? Once the patient is stabilized and upstairs, it may be time for a diagnostic team to start working together. The same goes for a company that is suffering through a turnaround situation—it is command and control time.

Project Importance Not Worth the Effort

Collaboration is not always warranted. We've all worked on projects that were strategically unimportant, yet people spent a great deal of time, effort, and other resources trying to complete them. It doesn't matter how well a collaborative group works together or how many innovative ideas they come up with if the outcome does not change something in a significant way. If the outcome makes no meaningful difference, all the effort and resources that go into the project are only for the sake of collaboration itself.

As discussed in the first paragraph of this chapter, not every decision needs to be made by a collaborative effort. Some recurring issues do not rise to the level of being strategically important enough to spend the time required to collaborate. If a corporate marketing department needs to plan a small charity-type event, that department alone should just own the responsibility for planning the event. All of the C-level executives do not need to be bothered with the minutiae of the planning after the board of directors or executive committee has approved the event and the budget.

Little Chance of Significant Improvements or Achievements

Collaboration isn't free; if there will be no results, don't bother. Consider one of the biggest possible collaborative arrangements a company can pursue—mergers and acquisitions. Failed M&A are often the result of an attempt to collaborate to reach goals that are unrealistic, too large, too ill-conceived, and too time-constrained. Dozens of studies covering hundreds of companies across all industries show that although management wants the gains that consolidation and economies of scale should bring, the great majority of mergers and acquisitions—across all industries—do not live up to their promises. Often it starts with a spreadsheet model that implies that synergies exist; that two plus two will equal five. There is voluminous empirical evidence that two plus two usually equals less than five, and often, less than four. According to one source, "One-third of the transactions provided marginal returns, while only 17 percent provided substantial returns to shareholders." One expert summed it up well: "That's a staggering number. That means those organizations were better off before they merged than after they merged" (Interlink Management Consulting, n.d.).

The trouble is, it's not always clear at the beginning of a collaborative project that the goal is unrealistic or that the available group does not have sufficient knowledge or diverse enough skills to make a real contribution. That's why successful collaborations follow a carefully thought out process that begins with defining and agreeing on the goal, as well as determining what needs to be done for the goal to be achieved and what resources will be necessary to accomplish essential tasks. In the second half of this book, you will learn how a group can ensure that its goal is achievable before it has invested too much time, money, and other resources.

Lack of Necessary Authority or Support

Congress, presidential administrations, state legislatures, local governments, and other bodies are well known for forming collaborative groups made up of experts from a wide range of fields, tasking them to come up with innovative solutions to seemingly intractable problems—and then thoroughly ignoring any results that are not in line with their original motivations. University presidents, corporate directors and CEOs, and other leaders have an unfortunate tendency to do the same.

For collaboration to be successful, the group needs sufficient authority or the necessary support to either implement the results or ensure that they are implemented. Otherwise, the process, although interesting, is a waste of resources and time. Worse, it leaves people who were involved or have an interest in the innovation feeling frustrated and skeptical about the collaboration process and any future efforts.

The Department of Homeland Security has a list of the items that can be purchased with DHS funding. They also have a list of which programs fund which items. However, it has not been clear how local first responder agencies obtain the funding. Government bureaucracy was keeping Homeland Security appropriations from being effective because no one knew how to actually get the funding. A task force was formed as part of the Homeland Security Appropriations Act of 2010. They were charged with "making recommendations for all levels of government regarding disaster and emergency guidance and policy; federal grants; and federal requirements, including measuring efforts" and to "especially evaluate: which policies and guidance need updating, and the most appropriate process by which to update them; which grant programs work the most effectively and where programs can be improved, and the most appropriate way to collectively assess our capabilities and capability gaps" (Paddock, 2011).

One of the task force recommendations was improved coordination of the state administrative agencies that administer security programs from different federal agencies. However, no further clarification was made regarding how to interpret federal guidelines and pass through the funding. The states, which had been unwilling to release the funding as required before the formation of the task force, have no incentive to begin administering the program as designed. The task force identified problems and possible solutions. However, members acknowledged that they have no authority to implement any of the recommendations. Therefore, all of the problems remain and all of the solutions go unused, simply because the final element—the execution of the solution—was not in the scope of the task force's authority.

On any project, whether corporate or otherwise, executive buy-in from the outset is important. There should be a clear business case from the outset that can be understood from bottom to top. Before embarking on a project, executives should conduct up-front planning and establish the semblance of a team that has authority to manage the collaboration process and implement some results.

Lack of Sufficient Diversity

Imagine that a family physician diagnoses you or someone close to you with osteoporosis and then collaborates with several similar internists on a treatment plan. That collaborative group would be unlikely to come up with the best results. For a comprehensive treatment plan, the group members need diversity—perhaps a dietitian, who can provide advice on special dietary needs; a physical therapist, who can prescribe exercises to help ameliorate the condition; a bone density specialist; other specialists, such as endocrinologists, rheumatologists, and orthopedic surgeons; and maybe someone who specializes in pharmacology or holistic health alternatives. Each of those people would bring to the table special knowledge, expertise, experience, and perspectives that the others lack so that they could see the patient's situation from different angles and develop the optimum treatment plan.

In the same way, a group made up entirely of engineers, or marketing experts, or school superintendents, or individuals from only one end of the political spectrum will not have the differing experiences, knowledge, talents, skills, and perspectives needed to look at the situation from all angles. Any collaborative group needs a certain amount of diversity to achieve truly innovative results.

Misaligned Reasons for Participation

When participants in a collaborative effort have vastly different reasons for participation, projects often fail. For example, when money or potential resources are a goal, participants may focus more on who will benefit instead of identifying and working toward a shared goal. They may appear to be working toward a common goal when in fact they are angling for a selfish outcome that will encourage a shift in resources toward them at the end of the process. If team members are preoccupied with protecting turf from day one, they aren't likely to find a common purpose. As a result, if the very topic of the collaboration is raising money that will eventually be doled out, organizers must be very mindful of the potential for conflicts throughout the entire process. Even if money is not at stake, participants need to be in the room for positive and innovation-oriented reasons. For example, if participants are there merely to retain the status quo or to defend their departments, a positive outcome is unlikely. It is more likely that there will be constant defensiveness and disagreement. Each member of a collaborative team needs some level of buy-in regarding the reason for the project. They need to realize throughout the experience that it is worth the investment of time, attention, and enthusiasm to build something that they feel is worthy; something that a group can find binding and reciprocal.

A Collaboration of Bad Guys

One definition of collaboration is "the betrayal of others by working with an enemy, especially an occupying force" (Encarta, 2001). History teaches us that collaboration is not always used for the general good. When it's used for good ends, the results can be very good. When it's used for bad ends, however, the results can be very bad, because bad guys who understand the power of collaboration make difficult foes for society. Members of terrorist organizations, organized crime, and street gangs often collaborate efficiently and effectively, which makes them difficult to combat.

The terrorist Umar Farouk Abdulmutallab, on December 25, 2009, demonstrated what happens when bad guys collaborate better than good guys. The twenty-three-year-old Nigerian national attempted to blow up Northwest Flight 253 from Amsterdam to Detroit shortly before landing. Reports indicated that U.S. CIA agents had gotten information from Abdulmutallab's father expressing his concern over his son's newfound religious views. Although his name was added to the U.S. National Counterterrorism Center, it was not added to the FBI's Terrorist Screening Database that feeds the U.S. No Fly List, and his U.S. visa was not revoked. If the intelligence agencies had communicated better, it is highly unlikely that Abdulmutallab could have gotten onto the airplane. The bad guys are going to collaborate, so the good guys are going to have to collaborate even more effectively and efficiently.

Gang collaborations can teach companies some valuable lessons. Consider the story of two rival Los Angeles gangs joining forces—and making life difficult for the police. The Bloods and the Crips decided to collaborate and make money selling illegal drugs and weapons. This caused grave concern among law enforcement agencies and experts. The deal was striking because these two gangs had been sworn enemies. In fact, the collaboration was so vast that it cut across racial lines, which had previously been considered unthinkable by law enforcement officials.

This has caused immense problems for the police, who need to deal with illegal drugs and weapons from this collaboration. As long as the two gangs were enemies, to a certain extent they contained each other. Now they are working together and there is no opposing force, which makes it much tougher for the police to maintain order. "Now, instead of having 200 guys that are arch-enemies with 200 other guys, you have 400 guys working together against law enforcement," said the sheriff's detective, Mr. Lyons (Audi, 2009).

We can see that negative collaboration can be very dangerous and thus should be nipped in the bud. Companies also see many negative collaborative efforts, in the form of rival companies coming together or plans within the organization to bring it down. Such collaborations can be quite dangerous, and companies need to take adequate steps to contain them before the problem gets out of control.

Collaboration can also be used for corporate theft, insider benefits, or political gain. For example, disgruntled individuals or groups within an organization can collaborate to advance their own goals and benefit themselves through sabotage or by providing confidential information to the organization's competitors. Organizations need to recognize the ways in which collaboration can be used for such negative purposes and take steps to guard against it. Otherwise, it has the potential of bringing the organization down.

All promising ventures carry risks; otherwise, everyone would already be doing them. Innovation creates economic value, and it requires a tolerance for risk. The point is to be in a position to properly assess and understand the monetary implications. Then, before embarking on the journey, address every possible essential requirement.

5

COLLABORATION ESSENTIALS

*All great inventions emerge from a long sequence of small sparks;
the first idea often isn't all that good, but thanks to collaboration
it later sparks another idea, or it's reinterpreted in an unexpected
way. Collaboration brings small sparks together to generate
breakthrough innovations.*

—MIHALY CSIKSZENTMIHALYI, AUTHOR
AND PROFESSOR OF PSYCHOLOGY

The prerequisites for solid collaboration include having a group of individuals who are willing to make sacrifices and endure inconveniences to realize a common objective. There is no easy way to achieve the rewards of collaboration—participants must put in the necessary time and energy, pool their assets, share the accountability for outcomes, and overcome differences, sometimes surrendering their individual preferences. But when the process is successful, the outcome is more than the sum of the individual efforts—it is something new that provides value for everyone involved.

But what has to be there for a collaborative effort to achieve that outcome? In this chapter, we look at the four key components that distinguish the process of collaboration from other forms of working together: increasing the capabilities of others, sharing risks, sharing rewards, and sharing responsibilities. Then we examine some essentials that must be there for a collaborative team to succeed.

Increasing the Capabilities of Others

People or companies can work well together without their efforts rising to the level of collaboration. Think of the early-twentieth-century assembly line. There were many people working together to accomplish the common goal of producing some sort of complex finished product. Although they did work together in the same place, they were not collaborating. In many cases they usually did not even need to speak to each other to do their jobs and accomplish their common goals. Each worker's concern was doing his or her part of the process and then passing the product to the next person, who would then complete a different part, until the product was complete. Workers did not aim to increase the abilities of the next person in the process, but just did their own jobs and passed it on. They were often held accountable for the speed and quality of their task. This still happens all the time in offices, with workers isolated in their cubicles. Employees are sometimes working very diligently, and managers are constantly finding new ways to improve efficiency. Unfortunately, sometimes everyone is just working really hard to do the wrong things faster instead of doing the right things.

On the other end of the spectrum, consider the people who worked on the Human Genome Project. According to research scientist Adil Shamoo and ethicist David Resnik, contemporary research requires a great deal of collaboration among scientists. The additional knowledge and abilities that many scientific research projects require to answer questions can be provided through collaboration. Advances often are likely to come from scientists collaborating across disciplines rather than following their traditional roles (Northern Illinois University, 2005). More than one thousand researchers from around the world with knowledge in multiple disciplines worked on the thirteen-year Human Genome Project (Oak Ridge National Laboratory, 2000). One group, one country, or one discipline would not have been able to tackle the project and accomplish the goals. Combined efforts and building on the pool of knowledge as the collaboration progressed enabled all of the participants to contribute more and make the project more successful. The issues they are dealing with are monumental, and their results are already revolutionizing the ways we diagnose, treat, and even prevent a number of diseases.

Shared Risks, Rewards, and Responsibilities

In other forms of working together there is often little or no sharing of risks. However, in true collaboration, a failure by one participant is usually shared by many others in the collaboration. That being said, in order to maximize innovation, the participants must be willing to try something that might fail. Actually, they must to be willing to try *many* things that might fail, if they really want to learn and achieve the best results possible. The mistakes involved in attempts, even failed attempts, ultimately lead to learning and become sources of new information. There is a great line in Mark Twain's *Tom Sawyer* that illustrates this: "But, on the other hand, Uncle Abner said that the person that had took a bull by the tail once had learnt sixty or seventy times as much as a person that hadn't, and said a person that started in to carry a cat home by the tail was gitting knowledge that was always going to be useful to him, and warn't ever going to grow dim or doubtful." Mistakes, when captured and internalized, teach people how to do things better in the future; mistakes are an essential component of experience.

Just as with risks, the rewards of collaboration are shared by other participants. If they accomplish their goal, they all share in the pride of accomplishment and the rewards that may come with success. The very fact that risks and rewards are shared evenly means that all participants have an equal responsibility to each other to try to make the collaboration successful. The individuals cannot consider themselves individually.

In basic chemistry, students learn about mixtures and solutions. It doesn't even take a chemist to realize that oil and water don't mix; there are some things we don't even attempt to make work together. A truly collaborative group can be thought of as a solution (that is, a liquid) with an even concentration (of risks, rewards, and responsibilities) throughout the system. For example, consider combining sugar in water versus sand in water. Sugar dissolves and is distributed throughout the glass of water. The sand sinks to the bottom. The sugar water could be considered a solution. The sand water is a mixture. The sand can be easily separated from the water because both still retain their individual characteristics. The sugar and the water have formed something new and different, and the parts cannot be differentiated, just as the individual contributions or responsibilities of collaboration cannot be separated out.

Essentials for Collaboration Success

For a collaboration to be successful, many elements must come together:

- Ongoing communication
- Willing participation
- Brainstorming
- Teamwork
- A common purpose
- Trust
- A plan for achieving the goal
- A diverse group
- Mutual respect
- A written agreement
- Effective leadership

Let's take a closer look at each of these.

Ongoing Communication

Open, effective communication and interaction among group members is the hallmark of successful collaboration. People need to talk with one another freely and regularly, to share information, knowledge, and ideas, and to keep the project moving forward toward their common goals. Groups that do not have this kind of interaction are nothing more than loose collections of individuals working on their own tasks, toward their own ends.

Before the advent of electronic and wireless communication, collaboration was actually more costly because participants needed to spend a great deal of time face-to-face, so they could share information and build on one another's ideas. The technology evolution that is still occurring is dramatically decreasing the costs of collaboration. Before our current technology made communication easy, group members needed to either be located relatively close to one another or spend a great deal of time traveling if they needed to collaborate in real time. Technology changed everything. Although it's still important for people to have opportunities to meet one another in person, today's collaborative groups use a wide range of technological tools to help them communicate with one another regularly and efficiently, even when members are in different locations and different time zones.

Willing Participation

Successful collaborations require a high level of commitment from every member of the group. But where does commitment come from? What would make you commit to a process that you know will take a great deal of time and effort? The most important factor may well be that you believe your effort will pay off, both for you and for your organization. Ideally, every member of the group is there because he or she *wants* to be there. Everyone believes that all are working toward the same, mutually beneficial goal and that each one of them will have gained something valuable when that goal has been achieved.

In the real world, however, some members of a collaborative group may be there not because they volunteered but because someone else—perhaps their boss—volunteered them, and this can cause problems for the group. Researchers who have studied the use of collaboration among parents, teachers, and administrators to improve schools found it is crucial that individuals participate in collaboration on a free and voluntary basis—because it is their choice. Forcing someone to participate in a collaborative project may mean that the attempt to manage the person's participation will end up sidetracking the group's focus: the person's resistance can end up distracting the rest of the group and hurting morale. In fact, one of the study participants used the term "clobberation" to describe participation that is actually directed or required by others. The study found that successful collaboration "was usually the result of collaboration that was voluntary while collaborative activity that was imposed by others often resulted in participants expressing feelings of frustration, betrayal, uselessness, cynicism, disappointment, pain and anger" (Slater, n.d.). There is a difference between forced volunteering and willing participation. The willing participant will add value, but the forced participant will not.

Brainstorming

We've all had the experience of struggling with a problem and then, once we finally found the solution, looking back and thinking, *That was so obvious! Why didn't I see that in the first place?* You didn't see the solution because it *wasn't* obvious—otherwise, you wouldn't have had the problem. As Einstein said, "We can't solve problems by using the same kind of thinking we used when we created them."

Brainstorming is the way that we get to the solutions and ideas that are not obvious at first glance—or even second or third. It's the creative part of the collaboration process, in which members of the group move beyond the "same kind of thinking" to come up with the new ideas that bring true value to the collaborative effort. Successful collaborative groups encourage everyone to imagine wildly and suggest as many ideas as possible, with the focus on quantity, not quality, reminding everyone that ideas that initially may seem outlandish or bizarre are, in fact, the path to innovation and progress. The more ideas on the table, the more likely the group will be able to move beyond established ways of thinking and come up with innovative ways to achieve their goal.

Brainstorming may be used to further the iteration sequence when a group is trying to solve a problem. Iteration is the act of repeating a process, usually with the aim of approaching a desired common goal. It's like building a cheerleading pyramid; each level makes the next level possible. If Bill, an individual, sits alone and writes potential solutions on a piece of paper, he may come up with some OK ideas. But if Bill, Mary, and Suzie sit in a room and each shares ideas, it is likely that one person's OK idea may trigger the next person's better idea. Here's a simple example: Bill says, "It would be great to have a vending machine in the office." Mary says, "It would be even better if it were a machine filled with healthy snacks, so everyone in the office can eat healthier." Bill then offers his thoughts about healthy eating, which encourages Mary to make more observations about the staff's eating habits. Then Suzie throws out another idea, suggesting they could all start a company-wide weight-loss and health competition. Then Bill remembers that the human resources department offers incentives for healthy lifestyle programs, and they realize that the company might even pay for the vending machine. As you see, none would have come up with the big idea alone, but as a group they iterated until the idea developed. The result of each iteration is used as the starting point for the next iteration.

At the TED conference in 2006, Peter Skillman, then design team leader at Palm, spoke of an experiment that showed the power of iteration. He compared the results of an experiment tested on two types of teams: kindergarteners and MBAs from top graduate schools. As part of the experiment, each group received spaghetti, string, and tape. Then each was given the goal of creating a free-standing structure to support a marshmallow. In most cases, the kindergarten kids scored higher than the MBAs. They showed some great lessons for collaboration—especially for the power of iteration. The MBAs often worked in parallel and tried to establish rules—seeking personal power instead of team success. The children just focused on the game as a team, without any real hierarchy. They made mistakes and performed many iterations, learning as a group from each one. Although it was a seemingly trivial game about a marshmallow, it definitely demonstrates the power of uninhibited iteration (Novogratz, 2006).

Iterations in a collaborative business project context may relate to the technique of developing ever-improving components in a brainstorming session. At a later stage in the process, they may help people work together to come up with better ideas for product development or process redesign. This process is well known to software developers, but it is very relevant to any innovation process, especially collaboration. Incremental iterative development is at the heart of a strong brainstorming process and the enhancement of the ideas that are derived from the process. The basic idea is that by repeating the cycles quickly, each person's new idea rapidly builds on—or springs off of—the previous idea.

Teamwork

As mentioned earlier, a true team is by definition a collaborative group. Groups of individuals may communicate with one another, participate in bringing a project to life, and generate new ideas in brainstorming sessions, but their process would not amount to collaboration in the absence of teamwork. It's teamwork that keeps people with a diverse set of skills, knowledge, information, and perspectives working together effectively and efficiently to achieve their common goal.

Dan Lyons, a former Olympian rower, explained that in the sport of rowing, the team cannot win, no matter how great the individual athletes, if only four of the team members row the first half of the race and the others row the last half. They must function as one in order to achieve their goal (Mergen, 2004). The concept is the same for a collaborative team. Unlike a rowing team, not everyone will always be working simultaneously. But all the team members need to participate fully in the entire process for the team to achieve its common goal.

A Common Purpose

You already know that the key element that defines a collaborative effort is a unifying, shared, meaningful goal. It's that common goal that brings all the team members together and gets them to commit the necessary time, energy, and resources.

It's all too easy, however, for the parties on a collaborative project to assume that they have a shared goal when in fact they each have a somewhat different understanding of what they are trying to achieve. Consider a group of friends who decide to collaborate on a cohousing community. Some might assume that their goal is to create a community in which everyone will have meals together in a common kitchen and watch over one another's children; others might assume that the goal is to find or build low-cost housing with some common areas in which people can congregate when they want to socialize. If the group moves forward too quickly without taking the time to clarify their goal and make sure that everyone is in agreement about what it is, they will undoubtedly run into huge disagreements that are likely to tear the effort apart.

Thus one of the first steps that a collaborative group must take is to invest whatever time is needed to clarify and align the goal. As the project proceeds, they also need to review their goal regularly to make sure that everyone is still heading toward the same destination.

Trust

How willing are you to share information and ideas freely when you are working with strangers? If you're like most of us, when you are working on a collaborative project, you need to know something about the other people first. You need to feel confident that they are putting the group's shared goal—not their own interests—first, and that they will keep confidential or sensitive information within the group, take you seriously, respect your point of view, and not take credit for your ideas.

That's why, along with defining and aligning the shared goal, an important initial step for a collaborative group is to establish trust. Lack of trust is one of the main reasons that many collaborations fail to achieve their goals. Without trust, people may hoard knowledge and hesitate to share their expertise and ideas with the group. Only when people feel comfortable and secure can they participate fully. Trust comes from making sure that everyone is working toward the same, shared goal, believes it is worthwhile, and knows the benefits of achieving it; when all team members believe their participation in the process is valued and necessary; and when people respect one another and the collaboration process.

A Plan for Achieving the Goal

Wikipedia is one of the best examples of collaboration, but many organizational development people find its collaborative structure puzzling. On the face of it, it appears not to have a structure; there is no leader, no institution, and no substantial organization. Yet it is obviously collaborative, and it is hard to argue with its success. If you look up "Wikipedia" in Wikipedia, you'll see that it is used by 365 million readers and contains over 18 million articles that have been written collaboratively by volunteers, and almost all of its articles can be edited by anyone with access to the site. Dig deeper and you'll see that although it appears to be the wild west, it is anything but. It has ingeniously exchanged the traditional institutional methods of managing collaboration for virtual replacements. It substitutes many of the tools we describe in the real, absolute, or physical world with alternates from the virtual world. There are rules of engagement on editing, content, and licensing. There are reasons for participation, common goals that the users are striving for. There are requirements about how the team is built (that is, who can participate), how topics are covered, and the quality of writing. Just like in the physical world, reliability, trust, and honesty are managed—but in the virtual world they are managed with rules and technology instead of humans in meetings. Privacy issues are addressed; power structures, recognition, and the concepts of community mirror those of the physical world. In some respects we see similar attributes when people interact on eBay, Facebook, LinkedIn Groups, Twitter, and other new social media.

If you attempt to collaborate with the idea of just getting a group of people together and winging it, you are likely to fail. That's because the people involved in a collaborative project need a clear purpose and direction, so they know where they are going and how they are going to get there. Everyone needs to be working from the same script, clearly understanding roles and responsibilities, and they need to have the same understanding of what success looks like.

Successful collaborative outcomes are the result of careful planning. A project might begin casually and informally, perhaps with a conversation between a few people who are interested in solving the same problem or in creating something altogether new. But it is unlikely to get very far without a plan, a framework in which participants can each apply their intellect to help make innovations happen. A well-developed plan

- Clarifies the goal and describes what needs to be done to achieve it
- Assigns roles and responsibilities
- Establishes a timeline
- Identifies necessary resources
- Describes the ways in which people will communicate and work together and how they will resolve conflicts

Conflict is an important part of the process, but it can be destructive instead of productive if the parties allow conflict to be focused on the people rather than on their ideas. To avoid conflicts that can end up tearing the group apart, all the parties need to discuss, understand, and be comfortable with their differences and commonalities, establish some ground rules, and decide on a process for handling conflicts when they occur. Plans should be realistic, flexible, and adaptable. Plans are likely to need adjustments as the group progresses toward its goal, but the basic framework has to be in place before work begins.

A Diverse Group

Diversity is the power behind collaboration. The Indian philosopher and environmental activist Vandana Shiva (1993) refers to the lack of diversity as a "monoculture of the mind" that reduces the number of perspectives and eliminates richness. The American journalist James Surowiecki (2004) has written about cognitive diversity that is achieved by choosing team members with differing backgrounds.

Without diversity, groupthink sets in. "Groupthink," a term originally coined by business author and editor William Whyte, describes a behavior you may have seen or even been a part of—one in which members of a group avoid conflict and expedite consensus by choosing not to test, analyze, and evaluate ideas critically. The most well-known example is the 1957 film, *Twelve Angry Men*, which tells the story of a jury that is ready to come in with a guilty verdict without discussion, based on their personal assumptions and prejudices, when they are challenged to examine the facts by a single holdout (played by Henry Fonda).

"Unfortunately, groupthink isn't just the stuff of compelling movies," says Sharon Allen, chairman of the board of Deloitte LLP. In business organizations opportunities for groupthink abound, from the shop floor to the C-suite. Allen says the story illustrates the importance of being willing to "consider new ideas, ask tough questions and enable every voice in the room to be heard. . . . Historians have cited [groupthink] as a prime suspect behind a diverse array of events including Pearl Harbor, the space shuttle *Challenger* explosion, the dot-com meltdown, and the collapse of Enron." Groupthink is often cited as a cause of the subprime mortgage debacle and financial crisis that triggered the recent Great Recession.

Yale research psychologist and UC Berkeley professor Irving Janis says that groupthink occurs "when the [group] members' strivings for unanimity override their motivation to realistically appraise alternative courses of action" (Janis, 1972, pp. 8–9). Groupthink can lead people to set aside any doubts or concerns they may have and make decisions without critically testing, analyzing, and evaluating the options. Instead of engaging in the free and open discussion that is essential to collaboration, the group members yield to the temptation to minimize conflict and reach consensus or unanimity without adequately considering the alternatives.

When groupthink begins to infect the group, their goal may become to achieve consensus, not matter what the cost. Individual creativity, uniqueness, and independent thinking can be advantages when making decisions as a group, but those advantages are lost when the members of the group do not feel free to voice opposing thoughts and instead pursue cohesiveness and avoid promoting any opposing viewpoints.

Groups that have not clearly defined a decision-making process that includes a mechanism for analyzing options are more susceptible to groupthink. Groupthink often seems to occur when a respected or persuasive leader is present, inspiring members to agree with his or her opinion (Fritscher, 2008). Groupthink is also more common in groups whose members have similar perspectives—the more similar their outlooks, the less likely they are to raise questions that might break their cohesion (Surowiecki, 2004). In fact, a collaborative group that has fallen victim to groupthink may devalue diversity to the point of there being no reason to have a group at all because they are unlikely to come up with anything new. Groupthink is said to be the phenomenon that is responsible for otherwise intelligent and knowledgeable people making disastrous decisions.

Different educational and life experiences, interests, thought processes, background knowledge, work experience, skills, and expertise all contribute to the diversity that makes a team rich in terms of creativity. A team that lacks diversity may tend to come up with cookie-cutter ideas; the best results of collaboration are realized from combining the widest possible range of ideas. It is diversity that gives a team the unique perspectives needed to create truly innovative solutions.

Mutual Respect

Along with diversity in a collaborative group, mutual respect is critical. Members must have true appreciation for one another's strengths, experiences, and knowledge, even when—especially when—there are extreme differences of ideology and opinions. Mutual respect is essential if group members are to trust one another enough to share their ideas freely.

It's important to distinguish between respect and tolerance. People whose ideas are tolerated may be listened to politely, but their ideas will not be given serious consideration. Once someone feels that his or her ideas and opinions are not being valued, the person will not feel comfortable expressing ideas in the future. You may see a person as one of the seats at the table, but you've likely lost most of their value to the project.

For a collaboration to be successful, team members must encourage, listen to, and seriously consider all of the ideas suggested by others in the group, no matter how unworkable they might seem. After all, no one knows where an idea will take the group until it has been voiced, discussed, and weighed by everyone. Ideas that later prove viable seldom emerge fully developed, but even if they are ultimately discarded, they should be given deliberate thought. Even the act of evaluating and discussing an idea that the group finally decides is unworkable can lead, directly or indirectly, to other, more feasible concepts.

A Written Agreement

Again, it's important for any collaborative group to ensure that everyone has the same understanding of the goal and how it will be reached. A written agreement helps the group avoid misunderstandings and lack of clarity that could derail the process after everyone has invested a great deal of time, effort, and resources.

The agreement does not have to be exhaustive; it can—and indeed it should—be simple, no longer than a few pages. Even a simple document can help the group use its time and resources as wisely as possible and avoid problems that could interfere with its ability to achieve its goal.

A typical agreement describes the reasons for the collaborative project, the goal, the project scope, the time frame, and constraints and limitations. For example, an agreement should describe what information will be shared and any laws, rules, and regulations that may require consideration. It also describes who will be responsible for what, how the group will make decisions, how conflicts will be resolved, how money will be allocated and accounted for, and how confidentiality and ownership issues will be handled. The agreement is not written in stone; instead, it should be a living document that will change as the nature of the work, the relationships, and even the goal itself change over time.

Effective Leadership

Great leaders exist at every level and in every segment of society, from corporate executives to teachers, charity coordinators, moms and dads, and team coaches. Whether someone is running a country or overseeing a classroom, there are important principles that apply. Whether you are Gandhi, Rockefeller, Jeff Bezos, Bill Gates, or just the leader of a group of people setting out on a three-day hike to a mountain lake, leadership is critical. How do the hikers decide what to do when they have a choice of trails, when to stop for lunch, what to do when someone falls behind, or where to set up camp for the night? How do they keep one another's spirits up when they are drenched by a sudden rainstorm or someone has forgotten to pack his sleeping bag? What should they do if there is a dramatic emergency out in the middle of nowhere—with no cell coverage and the nearest medical assistance hours away? These are the kinds of things that are addressed by leadership.

Leadership, in this case, might mean that one person has the role of leader or guide. But that's not always so. The members of the group itself might take on those responsibilities as the different situations come up: "How about stopping here for lunch?" or "Which trail does everyone think we should take?" someone might say to initiate a group discussion. Nevertheless, whether one person has been formally designated as the leader or the group is self-led, leadership of some sort is essential to keep the group focused on its destination and facilitating the process of getting there.

In the same way, a collaborative group needs leadership. A formal group usually has a designated leader, although different individuals might fill that position at different stages of the project. Sometimes a team, like the hikers, may be self-led, with leaders emerging from the group as needed to provide direction, keep people engaged, facilitate discussions, guide the decision-making process, and help to resolve conflicts. In some new collaborative experiences that are occurring on the Web, there is a sense of invisible leadership, but it is still leadership even when community-led. A group needs leadership, whether formal or self-determined. Without leadership, the participants can lose sight of their goal, go off on tangents, get bogged down in trivial matters, even disintegrate in the face of obstacles.

Each of these essentials must be present to effectively make it through the challenges of collaboration. If there aren't visible challenges, then we should question whether the topic even matters or whether the team members are even going through the stages of collaboration that we'll examine in the next chapter. Each stage presents certain trials and tribulations that will spark progress toward the rewards of a successfully realized goal.

6

STAGES OF COLLABORATION

Planning is bringing the future to the present so that you can do something about it now.
—ALAN LAKEIN, WELL-KNOWN
TIME MANAGEMENT AUTHOR

Collaboration begins with a problem or an idea, something you cannot achieve on your own. For example, if you (the country of Chile) do not have the expertise to rescue trapped miners, you have to reach out to anyone in any country who might be able to help. If you (a CEO) want to make your company more green, or you (a university president) want to find innovative ways of dealing with budget cuts, you can reach out to others who have the knowledge, expertise, and ideas to help you come up with innovative solutions and ideas. But no matter what triggers your collaborative effort, it is likely to consist of certain stages that take you and your colleagues from the initial idea to a successful outcome.

The Stages of Collaboration: An Overview

Every collaborative undertaking is different. Some are carefully planned, whereas others seem, from the outside at least, to happen out of nowhere. But few projects achieve worthwhile goals without purposeful preparation. Although some collaborations can succeed with little obvious planning and structure, the vast majority of those that succeed follow the same essential three-stage pattern.

During the first stage of a collaboration, the group gets started, defines its goal, and develops a plan for achieving the goal. In the second stage, the team implements the plan, monitors its progress, and revises the plan as needed. Finally, in the third stage, the group evaluates the outcome to see how well it met their criteria of success and decides what, if anything, to do next.

The three stages of a collaboration usually involve the key tasks listed here and described in the rest of the chapter. Not every collaborative project requires every action, of course, and tasks are not always done in the order shown here. But each collaborative effort has a greater chance of success when most or all of the steps are fulfilled and done well.

The First Stage: Getting Started

- Assembling the group
- Selecting or identifying a leader
- Defining and agreeing on the goal
- Identifying measures of success
- Establishing roles and responsibilities
- Agreeing on a working process
- Establishing a process for communicating with one another
- Setting priorities
- Making decisions

- Holding one another accountable
- Developing an action plan for achieving the goal

The Second Stage: Implementing the Plan

- Tracking and monitoring progress
- Revising the plan, if necessary

The Third Stage: Evaluating the Outcome

- Determining what worked and what might have been done differently
- Deciding on next steps

Getting Started

The way in which a collaboration gets started can determine whether it succeeds or fails. Groups that pay careful attention to the components at the early stages are more likely to be able to handle obstacles, stay focused on their goal, and come up with truly innovative ideas.

Assembling the Group

Although preexisting teams can and do collaborate, most collaborative ventures require assembling a group whose reason for being is to accomplish the unifying goal. Sometimes the group must be assembled very quickly, as in the successful rescue effort in October 2010 that saved the lives of thirty-three Chilean miners who had been trapped underground for sixty-nine days after their mine collapsed. Obviously this collaboration was not anticipated, but no time was wasted, due to the urgency of the situation. Egos were set aside as governments, companies, and individuals came together to try to accomplish the seemingly impossible task. Their efficient and effective collaboration undoubtedly saved the lives of the men and serves as an example of the way a collaborative effort should happen and the extent to which abilities can be enhanced by collaborating with others in the pursuit of a clear common goal.

Chile's state-owned mining company looked worldwide for the best equipment for each step of the rescue process. The cable that carried the Chilean-designed rescue capsule back up to the surface came from Germany. The drill rig and specially developed bits were from the United States. The video equipment was from Japan. Drilling experts from the United States went to Chile to make sure the drilling went well. NASA was also contacted by the Chilean government for advice on construction of the rescue pod and how best to feed the men while they were underground.

Compare Chile's willingness to collaborate, resulting in the rescue of all thirty-three trapped miners, with the complete lack of willingness to accept any sort of help exhibited by Russia in 2000 with the Kursk submarine tragedy. Russia refused assistance from the United States and the UK. Of course, there is no way of knowing whether accepting help would have saved any of the 118 men aboard, but by Russia's refusing all assistance until four days after the submarine explosions and grounding on the sea floor, the fate of the crewmen was sealed. There was no time to assemble an effective rescue team, and there were no survivors.

A pit crew working on a race car must be efficient in their execution when working together as a collaborative team. As a matter of fact, there are several companies that offer leadership and team building training using real race cars—delivering something similar to a real race car pit crew experience—to teach employees how to interact more collaboratively. The pit crew members must share the responsibility of their job with the others. If the jack man, the tire changer, or tire carrier do not do their job well, the whole team will fail. They also share in the reward when they all do well. The experience of functioning as a pit crew demonstrates how well the team can perform when they function as one unit.

Once your collaborative group has been assembled, it's a good idea to write a concise statement that describes the scope of the project. This helps to ensure that everyone involved has the same understanding of why the project was launched and what it intends to achieve, so any misunderstandings can be clarified before proceeding. One example of a short statement of scope for a large project is President John F. Kennedy's at the launch of the Apollo Project: "I believe this nation should commit itself to the goal of sending a man to the moon before the end of the decade and returning him safely to Earth." This statement of scope kicked off a project that cost in excess of $50 billion and lasted for more than ten years.

Selecting or Identifying a Leader

Contrary to the often-mischaracterized warm fuzzy notion of collaboration, these kinds of projects need disciplined and proficient leadership and management to be successful. Good leadership can add tremendous value to a collaborative effort by drawing together the team's vision, the members' belief in this opportunity for success, and the team's ability to make the impossible happen. Each individual brings a wealth of knowledge, skills, and expertise to the table, and a good leader will be able to channel and harness these for the benefit of the team.

The right leadership can be counted on to:

- Establish a vision of the future
- Enlist others to embrace the vision
- Create change
- Unleash the energy and talent of contributing members

Groups find their leaders in various ways. The leader might be the person who had the initial vision for the project. It might be someone who holds a position of authority. Leaders may emerge naturally or be selected by the group. For complex collaborative projects, the group might select a leadership team. Leadership might be rotated from time to time during a project—for example, some parts of the collaboration might be led by the group member who has the most expertise in that area.

No matter how they are selected, leaders of collaborative groups need certain traits that help them foster goodwill and trust among the team members, motivate people and spur them into action, provide people with direction, and harness the members' strengths and align them in the direction of the team's goals. Leaders need to be capable of listening attentively (which requires not doing much talking). They need to act as mediator and bridge to foster communication, to keep the project on track by constantly asking, "Okay, where do we go next and who's doing what?" Simply put, leaders are the glue that holds the group—and the project—together, making the best of available resources and everyone's talents, skills, and abilities to get everything done.

Groups have to be careful when selecting their leader or ceding leadership to someone who seems to be the natural choice. For one thing, the loudest voice in the room is seldom the most effective leader. Collaborative groups work best when led by leaders who are focused on the overall good of the project, not those who are most interested in control or power. Many teams will invariably be challenged by members who are accustomed to getting their way by browbeating others; this can slow progress, and good leaders will need the ability to manage through it. But if the leader himself is a bully with an intimidating style, any sort of innovation, whether through collaborative means or not, is likely to be hindered.

Leadership doesn't always have to be chosen in traditional ways. For example, effective leadership of collaboration efforts is necessary when dealing with disasters such as weather-related catastrophes or the results of terrorist attacks. Although groups need guidance, they do not always need a top-down designated leader—in some situations, the most effective leadership comes from the group itself. When the Midwest was struck by devastating tornadoes in 2011, many people organized themselves into efficient, self-led groups to collaborate on ways to deal with the disaster. That was in stark contrast to the government-led initial response to Hurricane Katrina, which most people would agree was not very efficient or effective. There was much criticism regarding FEMA and DHS not being able to coordinate the relief effort and the lack of leadership at all levels of government involvement.

Hierarchically selected leadership is more common in many business environments because the self-chosen leadership process, like that in the tornado example, is often misunderstood in the workplace. Just because it is an organic process doesn't mean it isn't a process. It is often based on a quick yet complex interaction where people essentially crowdsource the best leaders based on those with the most appropriate skill set to manage the issue at hand. In traditional crowdsourcing, you do an open call to an undefined group of people to gather those who are most fit to perform tasks. Even if you don't technically crowdsource, you can still get similar benefits when you focus on assembling leadership that has the most experience for the task. If identifying appropriate leadership for certain challenges becomes problematic, one simple way to get started is simply asking the group members one important question with regard to the particular issue: "Has any done this or anything like it before?" Leaders need skills and experience. Don't reinvent the wheel; take advantage of any prior experience people may have.

In the digital age, we see the possibility for increased collaboration during disasters using cloud computing applications that allow people to work together and help each other. Many websites—such as Snowmageddon, which was set up after a blizzard hit New York—offer a place for citizens to crowdsource information and notify each other of problems and any solutions that they have found. When the catastrophic 7.0 magnitude earthquake hit Haiti in January 2010, a group of graduate students at Tufts University in Boston and translators from a Haitian community in the United States gathered information about the most pressing needs and placed the coordinates on a map made available to rescue and relief teams. Simply knowing where to go to take which relief supplies or where security was needed maximized the efforts of the relief workers on the ground. Then, four days after the quake, one of the largest telecom companies in the country offered free short code text for relief efforts. The code allowed users to send free messages regarding missing persons and emergency needs to a central information center (Nelson, 2011).

Defining and Agreeing on the Goal

If you don't have a planned destination when you embark on a journey, you can end up wandering the countryside until you find somewhere to stop. That's fine, if that's the kind of journey you intended. But if you want to get somewhere specific, you need to begin by defining your destination and then figure out how you will get there.

We're often told about the importance of goal setting to our personal lives, for everything from personal finances to diet and healthy lifestyle. The acronym "SMART" is often applied to goal setting, a reminder to make the goals specific, measurable, attainable, realistic, and timely. This applies to defining goals for collaborative groups too. The group's goal should be specific enough that it includes provisions for any special circumstances that might occur. Obviously, when applied to group goals rather than personal goals, the goal must also be agreed to within the group.

A collaborative venture always has a destination—a goal. After all, isn't reaching the destination—achieving the goal—the point of the whole thing? But many, if not most, collaborative ventures begin with a vague, ill-defined goal: *we want to improve health care for low-income people; we want a product that will outsell the iPad.* Those kinds of fuzzy goals can get you started. But little is likely to be accomplished unless your group clearly defines and agrees on the results they are trying to achieve. So one of the group's first tasks is to describe the goal in enough detail so that every member can agree: "Yes, that's exactly what we want to achieve." This process can take some time, but if you set off on the journey without defining and agreeing on the destination, the group is likely to waste a lot of time—in effect, wandering in the countryside without ever really getting anywhere.

It's not that the goal will remain unchanged as the group works, however. After all, the purpose of collaboration is to come up with solutions and ideas that people haven't thought of before. Who knows what will come up as ideas begin to fly? Your group's stated goal may be to develop a miniature, portable, wireless telephone. What if, along the way, you end up inventing the Palm Pilot or the BlackBerry? What if you get side-tracked altogether and instead develop the Sony PlayStation 3? Yet even if you end up revising the goal significantly, or even dropping it alto-gether in favor of a terrific new idea, the process of clearly defining the goal is what gets you started and allows you to dive into the free, open exchange of ideas that is so vital to the process.

Identifying Measures of Success

According to a 2004 study by the Standish Group, 71 percent of projects fail outright or are "challenged." One of the top four reasons cited is that the team had no clear criteria by which their results would be measured (Tuffley, 2004). Content and many procedures will be affected by the stated criteria. Therefore it makes sense that if the criteria are not clearly stated, the whole project will not be able to meet expectations.

In ancient Rome, huge obelisks showed pilgrims the way to the major basilicas, confirming that they had arrived at their destination. Measures of success similarly describe the way in which the collaborative group will know when they have reached their goal. When the group defines its goal at the beginning of the project, they also need to define the measures of success—exactly what they expect the successful completion of the project to yield.

Identifying the measures of success means describing the situation that will exist once the goal has been achieved. Coming up with that description helps the team focus its journey on its destination. It is also, in a way, a test of whether the goal is achievable.

To make sure that every member of the collaborative group knows how the results will be measured, the group needs to ask, "How will we know when we've achieved our goal? What will success look like?" The collabora-tive group formed to rescue the Chilean miners had a very clear goal and a clear measure of success. When the miners emerged from that pipe alive and in decent health, they knew they had achieved the desired outcome of their collaboration. When President Obama ordered the Navy Seals into

Pakistan on May 1, 2011, they also had a very clear goal and a clear measure of success: leave Pakistan with the physical body, alive or dead, of the al Qaeda leader. When they flew Bin Laden's body out of the country, they—and the world—knew that they had accomplished their goal.

Establishing Roles and Responsibilities

A key feature of a collaborative group is that every member has an important part to play in the process—otherwise, there's no reason for them to be there. In addition to identifying or selecting the right leader, the group needs to clearly establish what everyone's roles and responsibilities will be in helping to achieve the goal and decide how they will hold one another accountable. Identifying clear roles and responsibilities increases the chances that everything that needs to get done will get done. And there is another benefit as well: knowing that their contributions are essential for the project's success helps people stay engaged and increases their commitment. By the same token, you should remove people who will not add value. In many corporate settings, there are many extraneous people involved in projects. If you are attempting to break new ground, the talent in the room doesn't need to babysit the superfluous members. Every member must have the intellectual capacity, experience, desire, and talent to add real value.

Agreeing on a Working Process

No matter how worthwhile the goal, collaborative projects can easily fall apart if the participants have not agreed on a realistic process for working together. Among other things, that working process should be specific to the current collaboration and describe the process and the ways in which members will communicate with one another and external sources while involved in the project, set priorities, make decisions, deal with disagreements, handle conflict, hold one another accountable, and deal with unforeseen obstacles and changes in the situation. This document might be called an operating agreement, but whatever the document is called, its purpose is not legal in nature. It exists to provide guidelines to the group and minimize disagreements.

Establishing a Process for Communicating with One Another

Open, ongoing communication lies at the heart of the collaborative process. In fact, communication is so vital to a collaboration that poor communication among group members can lead to the failure of an entire project. Only by communicating often and freely will people be able to come up with new ideas and avoid problems that can derail the project.

A very important positive attribute of open and effective communication is that it creates a sense of belonging and trust among the team members. Ongoing communication also ensures that resources are being used wisely, people are not wasting time and energy duplicating one other's work, nothing essential is being overlooked, and minor problems are caught before they escalate into major obstacles.

Obviously, communication is easier when the collaborative group is an intact team of people who work together on a daily basis. But the members of collaborative groups are often scattered. Even within the same organization, people might work in different buildings, different cities, different states, and, increasingly, in different countries. Fortunately, we now have an increasingly sophisticated variety of technological tools— e-mail, instant messaging, video and conference calls, web-based meeting rooms, blogs, wikis, and Twitter—that allow collaborative groups to stay in touch no matter where in the world they are.

Even with—indeed, especially with—all those tools, it takes careful planning and special effort to manage the communication process to make sure that ideas and information do not disappear into the ether, people do not feel disengaged from the process, and minor problems do not balloon into unmanageable obstacles. The group needs to decide what tools to use; how often and under what circumstances they will communicate with one another; which types of communications need to go to everyone and which, if any, need to go only to subgroups; and what they will communicate about the project to those outside the collaborative effort. The communication process should also include making sure that everyone understands the effect of any financial constraints, rules, regulations, policies, or procedures on the outcome so that people will not waste time and energy on solutions that cannot be implemented.

Setting Priorities

The work involved in a collaborative effort takes time—and time is the resource that is most likely to be in short supply among members of the group. Although difficult, priorities must be established and adhered to. The Global Forum for Health Research concluded that failure to establish a process for priority setting created a situation of heavy economic and social cost in which only about 10 percent of health research funds from public and private sources was being devoted to 90 percent of the world's health problems (measured in DALYs, the overall measure of disease burden—number of years lost due to bad health, disability, or early death) (Tugwell et al., 2008). Although it sometimes seems counterintuitive when managers get lost in the trees of the greater forest, a reduction in the quantity of priorities accomplishes more than a multitude of priorities. The collaborative group should have a clearly defined priority.

Making Decisions

The group will have many decisions to make along its journey to the goal. Some of those decisions will be relatively minor, whereas others can have significant impacts, positive or negative, on the project outcome. The Rogers Commission found that NASA's organizational culture and decision-making processes had been a key contributing factor in the 1986 Space Shuttle *Challenger* disaster. There was a flaw in the O-rings that allowed a chain of events causing the space shuttle to disintegrate seconds after launch. NASA managers had known of the flaw and disregarded warnings of the safety risk (NASA, 1986). The incident is often used to illustrate groupthink, in which the group avoids the necessary decision-making process and seeks instead to reach consensus simply to minimize conflict.

Decision making will go much more smoothly if the group agrees on an appropriate process ahead of time. Is this going to be a democracy? An autocracy ruled by a trusted, benign dictator? Or will decisions be made only by consensus? Will members and/or the leader have authority to make certain decisions without consulting everyone? How will the group handle conflicts? What happens if not everyone agrees with a decision?

Holding One Another Accountable

The members of a collaborative group depend on one another for success. When people miss deadlines, fail to provide information or resources, delay returning calls or responding to e-mail, or otherwise neglect the tasks they agreed to carry out, everyone is affected.

It can be hard to hold people accountable. We all have trouble telling someone that they are letting us down. But to avoid delays, problems, frustration, bad feelings, and worse, the group needs to decide what must happen when someone isn't carrying out a key responsibility. It must be OK to remove people who are not adding value, and there must be a process for doing so.

Developing an Action Plan

Even if you have a clear destination in mind for a journey, if you lack a map, how will you know whether you are approaching the goal—or, indeed, straying away from it? Surely your objective in joining a collaborative effort is not to attend pointless meetings for months on end. If that happens, you will probably find good reasons to do other things instead.

A good plan of action, put in writing and agreed to by all parties in the collaboration, serves as a map of sorts, helping to keep the group on the path towards its goal. At a minimum, an action plan describes what, who, when, and what if; that is, *What will be done? Who will do it? When will it be completed?* and *What if we run into problems?*

An important part of developing an action plan is determining how progress will be measured. What milestones along the way can the group use to measure its progress—or lack thereof? Does the group need to schedule regular check-ins or meetings to make sure it's on track toward meeting its goals? What are some red flags that might indicate a need to call everything to a halt and reexamine the action plan—or even the goal itself?

Implementing the Plan

The old proverb states, "The proof of the pudding is in the eating." This holds true for your collaboration. As you put the plan into action, you start moving toward your goal, tracking and monitoring your progress, and revising the plan as needed along the way.

Tracking and Monitoring Progress

When you develop your action plan, you identify milestones for tracking the group's progress. But it's important not to wait for deadlines to see how things are going. Subgroups and individuals who are carrying out some of the tasks needed to achieve the goal need to keep everyone informed about their progress. That ongoing communication is essential to keep people in the loop, so that everyone knows what's happening and feels included in the effort, even at times when they do not have much to do themselves. This is also important for catching problems in their early stages, before they escalate into insurmountable obstacles.

Monitoring is an iterative process in which problems generate as much knowledge as the lack of problems. Whether an effort is a success or fails to accomplish the task at hand, it should be evaluated and tracked. Measurable indicators are important for monitoring a process, as they provide a checklist with which trends can be evaluated and tracked.

Revising the Plan, If Necessary

Collaborative projects—indeed, life itself—would go more smoothly if we could anticipate every problem ahead of time and if things never changed. But the one thing that we can nearly always count on is that things seldom work out quite as we anticipated, and they *will* change. It's much easier to handle surprises when we expect them, even if we can't know when they might happen or what they might be.

Although it is just not possible to anticipate everything (*What if there is a tsunami?*), the group should do its best when drawing up the action plan to anticipate surprises—*What if a key person has to drop out? What if we can't*

find some of the resources we need? What if there is a delay getting approvals?—
and come up with some strategies for dealing with them. As the project
progresses, the team needs to review the plan often and revise it in response
to new information and changes in the situation. In advance, expect that
unanticipated challenges will arise, and build processes to manage them.
Every unexpected obstacle can't become a deer-in-the-headlights moment.
One differentiator between a remarkable team and a mediocre team is that
great teams have the ability to plow through catastrophes and just keep
going. If you didn't expect some startling speed bumps along the way, you
shouldn't profess to be an innovator.

Evaluating the Outcome

Hindsight is the clearest sight of all. Even if the group plans to disband
after the project has been completed, debriefing the collaborative effort to
evaluate the outcome—successful or not—offers everyone involved a
sense of closure and helps them identify what they have learned that they
can use the next time around.

In the most positive outcome of the evaluation process, the parties determine that the collaborative process was so successful that they decide to
work together again—usually on something larger. For example, Shanghai
Pharmaceutical and Pfizer worked together to promote a vaccine that is used
in China to prevent diseases in toddlers and infants. It was successful
enough that it led to a more significant relationship. In April 2011, they
announced signing of a memorandum of understanding to jointly pursue
potential new business opportunities in China. The partnership would leverage Shanghai Pharmaceutical's established market presence in China with
Pfizer's global capabilities for innovative medicine development.

David Simmons, Pfizer's president and general manager, emerging
markets and established products, said, "Our intent to explore a range
of business opportunities with Shanghai Pharmaceutical is an example of
our commitment to expand our presence in China in collaboration with
the local industry. Shanghai Pharmaceutical has been one of Pfizer's

major partners in China for years and is currently our largest distribution customer in the market."

Lu Mingfang, Chairman of Shanghai Pharmaceutical, stated, "From our first partnership discussion with Pfizer, we were impressed not only with their capabilities, but also their thoughtfulness toward the Chinese market. The Chinese pharmaceutical market is very dynamic and we believe a company must be forward thinking to succeed in China. Shanghai Pharmaceutical is built off of a vision for what the Chinese healthcare market will become, not what it has been. We respect Pfizer's global experiences and resources and believe they are an ideal partner for us in the continuous evolution of our business model and implementation of an international strategy" (FiercePharma, 2011).

Determining What Worked and What Might Have Been Done Differently

Successful or not, it is important to assess each collaborative effort; the conclusion becomes a determining factor in how best to pursue the next one more effectively.

An evaluation, perhaps held as a group conversation or conducted as a survey, asks the participants to consider such questions as

- What worked?
- What might have been done differently?
- What did we learn that will help us work more efficiently and effectively the next time we join a collaborative effort?

Exploring those questions allows participants to gain value from the process even if the collaboration did not achieve the exact desired outcome, and it helps the group decide on the next steps.

Deciding on Next Steps

Will you implement any of the processes into any other aspects of your business? If something was learned during the collaborative effort, could it benefit an area that had not been considered initially? Did the collaboration result in anything that might be able to be further developed? For example, if the collaboration resulted in a Swiffer-type product, the next step might be to try adding more features, resulting in Swiffer WetJet or Swiffer Sweeper Vac.

Many big accomplishments have risen from the wisdom generated by previous disappointments. In fact, one of the fundamental principles of capitalism is that people and organizations can fail. The ones that are ultimately successful, though, learn from their failings and often go on to become platforms for big achievements. When examined, failure is one of the elements that set up future efforts for success—as we will see in Chapter Seven.

7

SETTING UP FOR SUCCESS

Develop success from failures. Discouragement and failure are two of the surest stepping stones to success.

—DALE CARNEGIE

There is a lot you can do to help your collaborative effort succeed. You can make sure that the essentials are in place. You can assemble the best team possible, seeking people with the right combination of knowledge, experience, abilities, and skills. You can contemplate early decisions very carefully, bring the group to a common understanding of the objectives, and develop realistic action plans for achieving goals. There are some tried and true strategies to improve the probabilities that you will see a return on the investment in time, energy, and other resources. According to Harvard professor and team expert Richard Hackman, research suggests that condition-creating accounts for 60 percent of the variation in how well a team eventually performs (Hackman, 2011). In other words, it is well worth investing extra effort in the setup stages. The old saying applies: "Failing to plan is planning to fail."

In this chapter, we'll examine what to consider when assembling your team, how to define and align the shared goal, what an action plan needs to include if it is to guide the group toward a successful outcome, and the decisions the group needs to make about its working process. In Chapter Eight, we'll look at strategies for making the collaborative process efficient and effective and for keeping people committed as you move together toward your common goal.

Assembling the Team

Even elementary school children know that choosing teams can be almost as important as the game you are actually playing. This process often becomes so turbulent that teachers step in to facilitate for the kids. Sports teams are notorious for spending big dollars to recruit the right combination of players. If you look at the Bowl Championship Series (BCS), you see that the top twenty-five schools each spent, on average, about $630,000 for recruiting during the 2009–2010 school year. Number-one-ranked Auburn spent $1.1 million. In the right combination, good players build teams that win games (Dosh, 2011). Each athlete is put on the team because that person has something to contribute to the team's ability to achieve its collective goal; otherwise, the athlete should not be there. Collaboration works best when every member has something unique to contribute to the group's success, and when any member who becomes unproductive is removed. Your team will be stronger if you look for people who have certain key traits and characteristics that work well in combination. The following are attributes that make good team members:

- A positive attitude, open-mindedness, curiosity, and enthusiasm for the subject

- Good communication skills

- Flexibility and the ability to tolerate ambiguity

- A willingness to take risks

- Critical-thinking and problem-solving skills
- Creativity
- The ability to be self-reflective
- Good interpersonal skills
- The ability to see the big picture

A Positive Attitude

A survey conducted by Mitch Ditkoff and Tim Moore of Idea Champions, Carolyn Allen of Innovation Solution Center, and Dave Pollard of Meeting of Minds also found that attitude counts for members of a collaborative group. According to the survey results, "Most people would rather have inexperienced people with a highly positive attitude than highly experienced people who lack enthusiasm, candor, or commitment." Survey respondents gave the highest rating to "*enthusiasm* for the subject of the collaboration and *open-mindedness and curiosity.*" They also indicated that "candor, courage and timeliness of follow-through are very important qualities in a collaborator, along with strong listening, feedback and self-management skills and diversity of ideas" (Ditkoff, Moore, Allen, & Pollard, 2005).

Good Communication Skills

It makes sense that good collaborators need to be excellent communicators. Without communication, there would be no collaboration. These days, a lot of interaction happens through electronic media, so team members need more than just traditional interpersonal communication skills such as active listening and adeptness at clarifying and giving constructive feedback. They must also be able to express themselves clearly in an e-mail, a chat room, on Skype, or in a Twitter message. Increasingly, they must also be able to communicate well in a multicultural context in which people have different native languages and cultural jargon and differing ideas about what and how to communicate.

Flexibility and the Ability to Tolerate Ambiguity

Some people feel more comfortable when things are black and white—when there is one right answer and one wrong answer; one right way of doing something and one wrong way of doing it. But collaboration comprises shades of gray—if there *were* one right answer or way of doing something, there would be no reason to collaborate. Thus the best collaborators are those who can be flexible and tolerate a certain amount of ambiguity as the team goes through the sometimes arduous process of trying to go beyond what they already know and discover something new.

In the second chapter of his book *What Matters Most*, Jungian analyst Jim Hollis states, "Certainty begets stagnation, but ambiguity pulls us deeper into life. Unchallenged conviction begets rigidity, which begets regression; but ambiguity opens us to discovery, complexity, and therefore growth. The health of our culture and the magnitude of our personal journeys require that we learn to tolerate ambiguity, in service to a larger life" (Hollis, 2008, p. 27). Similarly, collaborators need the intellectual curiosity, flexibility, and nimbleness to handle the unknown. They should consider uncertainties intriguing, not something to be feared.

There are some people for whom curiosity and flexibility is 100 percent immediate and natural—people who may start timidly but become energized by the opportunity. Then there are the people who simply do not have much intellectual curiosity. Those people prefer to follow more traditional paths because they may find venturing into uncharted territories too intimidating or at least not interesting to them.

A Willingness to Take Risks

Many people work best when they can clearly see the road ahead. They dislike change and feel uncertain or uncomfortable when things are not predictable. But collaboration is all about revelations that come from trial and error—it's that very unpredictability that makes it possible for the group to take the flying leaps needed to come up with truly innovative results. A collaborative team is strongest when its members are bold enough to try different ideas to make changes and are willing to take those leaps.

There are ways to increase comfort levels when the troops get into unknown territory. For example, analogies are a great tool for helping people feel more secure and therefore more productive. You can find analogies in sports, relationships, children, celebrities, and books that help people find a frame of reference and gain confidence. Analogies need not be trite or even from reality. A scene from a movie might resonate and inspire more than a business analogy will. Businesspeople have successfully drawn inspiration and confidence from scenes in the *Indiana Jones* and *Rocky* franchises and from *Forrest Gump*, *Braveheart*, and *Field of Dreams*, to name just a few.

Critical Thinking and Problem-Solving Skills

People who are good at interpreting, analyzing, and evaluating information and ideas in terms of the context and the goal make excellent members of a collaborative team. These are the people who can see the connections among all the multiple factors that may be involved in the situation, including applicable rules and regulations, policies, politics, financial considerations, the potential results of various paths of action, and more. Without these kinds of abilities among its members, a group risks coming up with unrealistic and unworkable options. It is unlikely that each member of the group will have these kinds of skills to the same degree, but there is a minimum level that is acceptable; otherwise, you risk dragging the group down to the lowest common denominator and slowing down the process. By the same token, bringing the highest-level people—those with world-renowned competencies—in for simple tasks can be like using a howitzer to rid the kitchen of ants; it is way more firepower than you need, and it could get messy.

Creativity

When we think of creativity, we usually think of people who work in some aspect of the arts. It's true that creativity is a prerequisite for success if you want to be an artist, a playwright, a composer, or a choreographer. But we've all had those "aha!" moments, when a brilliant new idea or a solution to a problem appears out of nowhere. Creativity simply refers to the ability to come up with something that did not exist before—which is, after all, the objective of a collaboration. Thus the more collective creativity the group possesses, the better chance they have of coming up with something entirely new.

Williams Pipeline, a $20 billion energy company whose stock was taking a beating during the telecommunications boom, had an experience that illustrated the importance of including people from many different organizational levels and functions to inspire creativity in the group. At a routine meeting to discuss their gas pipelines business, someone brought up the drop in the company's stock price, and it was attributed to the fact that many other competitive companies were adding telecom to their portfolios. A maintenance worker, there to add his perspective regarding the old pipeline infrastructure, served up an idea: "Why not put fiber optic cables in our old pipelines?" That innovative suggestion from someone who saw things with very different eyes was the origination of a new part of Williams' business that at one point created billions of dollars in shareholder value.

The Ability to Be Self-Reflective

People who have a good understanding of their strengths and weaknesses are more likely to be able to understand the ways in which they can best contribute to the collaborative effort. They are also more likely to be able to tolerate the often intense exchange of ideas and opinions that are part of the process without withdrawing or becoming defensive.

When people are venturing into unknown territory, working with unknown people, sharing or opening up in ways that are different, they need to check their egos at the door and recognize that some people are better than they are at certain things (whether by training, experience, or inclination).

Good Interpersonal Skills

Because collaboration is an extended series of interactions that require working closely with other people, the best collaborators are people with good interpersonal skills. They are aware of and able to manage their own feelings while tuning in to the feelings of others. They can "read between the lines," as it were—body language, facial expressions, tone of voice, even the tone in an e-mail message—to sense when someone means more, or less, than they are saying. They can give and receive feedback in a non-threatening way by focusing on issues, not on personalities.

Poor interpersonal skills that lead to interpersonal tension can result in a breakdown of the collaborative effort. This happens when people are insensitive to the feelings of others, are more concerned with posturing and winning than with building relationships, and prefer to do things on their own and in their own way. Conversely, the best collaborators enjoy the connections and the interchanges with others. They like hearing, considering, and discussing other people's ideas and rationales. They are able to listen attentively to others, ask questions to fully understand what is being said, and remain respectful even if they ultimately disagree with what has been suggested.

The Ability to See the Big Picture

Most businesspeople have worked on projects in which their colleagues got so caught up in the details that they seemed unable to distinguish between what was important and what was not. When people lose sight of the big picture—the overriding goal that drives the collaborative effort—they can easily lose steam, becoming frustrated by minor problems, waste time on things that do not need to be done, or get distracted by other priorities.

It takes a goal—one person's or a group's—to get a collaboration started. Then it needs to be shared with and accepted by the larger group so everyone's efforts can be directed toward achieving the same end. Internalizing the goal is what helps the group remain focused on the big picture during the difficult times and work through problems together to achieve success.

There are many versions of the parable of the blind men and the elephant, which is believed to have originated in India. Basically, a group of blind men wanted to learn what an elephant looked like, so they went to touch the animal. One man touched its side; another, its tail; another, its tusk; the next, its leg; still another, its ear. When the men got together to talk about the elephant, which they could now "see" in their minds, there was no agreement whatsoever. They described the animal to the others as being like a wall, a rope, a pipe, a tree, and a hand fan. They were each partially correct, but because they did not see the big picture and would not listen to the others, they all ended up being completely wrong. The lesson is clear.

Defining and Aligning the Goal

Imagine what would happen if each of the players on a baseball team had a different idea of the goal and a different sense of its importance? Chances are that team wouldn't win very often, if at all. The players would be working at cross-purposes instead of together; some would have a high level of commitment to the game, while others might not bother to show up when they had something better to do.

Commitment to a collaborative project comes from a shared, unifying goal. It's the commonality of the goal that propels the project forward and keeps people going when the going gets rough. Thus, one of the first things that your collaborative group needs to do is make sure that everyone (1) has the same understanding of what that goal is and (2) agrees that it is worth the effort. Here are some ways to do that.

Include Everyone in the Goal-Setting Process

People have an inherent need to be part of the solution. There is a great story about the care that General Mills took in designing its Betty Crocker cake mixes. They'd been espousing speed and ease in the kitchen since 1931 with products like Bisquick; they launched the cake mixes in 1952, almost two decades later. The company called on the market research of Dr. Burleigh Gardner and Dr. Ernest Dichter, both business psychologists. The problem, according to psychologists, was that the mixes made the process too easy and simple. Dichter, in particular, believed that powdered eggs, often used in cake mixes, should be left out, so women "could add a few fresh eggs into the batter, giving them a sense of creative contribution" (Brignull, 2009).

As a result, General Mills altered the mixes, eliminating the powdered egg. The requirement to add eggs at home was marketed as a benefit, conferring the quality of "homemade" freshness and authenticity on the boxed cake mix. And it worked; Betty Crocker cake mixes became the industry standard. Their success demonstrates how people need to feel that they have made a real contribution to the achievement of the goal.

Collaborations are also more successful when everyone is involved in the goal-setting process. Collaborations often begin with the idea of one individual or a small group who then assemble a team to work on the project. In many cases, those with the idea present it to the team in the form of an already-formulated goal. They get tacit agreement and then launch the project, full steam ahead, only to find that it's not long before people start to peel away, pleading other commitments. To get the true buy-in that keeps people involved from start to finish, every member of the collaborative group needs to be fully involved in the process of defining and agreeing on a mutual goal that is worth achieving for all the parties.

Discuss, Clarify, and Refine the Goal

When people gather around a common purpose, everyone brings a different frame of reference to the table. What seems obvious to one person or group may not be obvious to the others—or even on their radar. It's as if everyone is looking out of a different window on a different floor of a building—the scenes they describe may be similar, but they won't be the same.

Getting everyone to the same window on the same floor takes time. The group needs to discuss, clarify, and revise the goal until everyone has the same understanding of what it is and agrees that it accurately expresses what they are all trying to achieve—their reason for working together in the first place. Without that common understanding and full agreement, you might as well not bother.

Put the Goal in Writing and Share for Review

Remember the old telephone game? One person whispers a little story to the next person in a circle, who whispers it to the next person, and so on. By the time the story gets back to the first person, it has usually changed significantly. The tendency for the message to get changed in the course of verbal communication is why we put contracts, agreements, and other important information in writing.

The act of writing may seem like a superfluous step after the group has thoroughly discussed and agreed on its unifying goal. But a written goal helps to avoid misunderstandings, and the act of writing down the goal goes a long way toward ensuring clarity and cohesion when you launch the project.

Not only does writing down the goal help ensure that everyone is heading for the same destination, but it also serves as a focal point during the project, a reminder of the group's reason for being that can be invoked if things seem to be going off track. When differences begin mounting, the written goal statement can be the squabble solver.

The goal should be written as simply, concisely, and as clearly as possible and distributed to each member. The group should continue to refine the goal statement until everyone agrees that it accurately describes the intent of the project.

Developing an Action Plan and Agreeing on a Working Process

Before starting work on the project, the group needs to ask itself a great many questions and make some very important decisions: what actions they will take to achieve their goal and what process they will follow to work together effectively. Making these decisions requires an investment of time that will pay dividends later. These decisions also affect everyone, so everyone needs to be involved in the decision-making process.

There will be some crossover between the action plan and the working process. The product of the group's discussions will be two separate documents, but the discussions will move back and forth between the two. What's important is that the group come up with both an action plan and a working process, write them down, and get everyone's agreement before they launch the project.

The Action Plan

The action plan is the map that will guide the group on its journey toward the goal. This map is crucial to a successful outcome. The project can founder or even fail if, for example, things are not finished, or are incorrectly completed; deadlines are not realistic; or no one has bothered to think about where to obtain essential resources. There are questions to be considered when developing an action plan, including:

- What tasks need to be done to achieve the goal?
- Who will do what and when?
- What material resources (space, equipment, money, and so on) will be needed? Where and how will we get them?
- What human resources outside the group are needed to make this project successful? How will we obtain the support and buy-in needed from these people?
- How will we monitor and track our progress?
- What dangers need to be considered? What safeguards need to be put into place?
- What problems are we likely to encounter, and how will we handle them if they occur?
- What would make us stop and rethink what we are doing?

The action plan should be put in writing, revisited as often as necessary to make sure that the project is on track, and revised or even rewritten when circumstances change. Throughout the process it should be clear what needs to be done to achieve the goal, what resources have been or are being used, what success has been achieved as measured against the time-line, and whether each person's responsibilities are being met.

The Working Process

In addition to developing a workable action plan, the group needs to decide on a process for working together. The time they devote to coming up with that process will pay off in terms of reducing misunderstandings, confusion, and unproductive conflict down the line.

The discussions to come up with a working process should cover all or some of the following:

- The scope of the project, along with any constraints, limits, and boundaries, including applicable governing laws, rules, and regulations

- The roles and responsibilities of everyone involved in the project

- How and when group members will communicate with one another

- The process by which the group will resolve conflicts and make decisions

- Ground rules to govern the ways that people work together

- Details of budgeting for the project, including how money will be allocated and accounted for

- How and when reports will be prepared and who will receive them

- What will remain confidential and how confidentiality issues will be handled

- How materials, resources, or information will be transferred and who will ultimately hold title or ownership

- How the products of the collaborative effort, such as products and inventions, will be managed, owned, and licensed, and what can or cannot be published

Like the action plan, the working process should be written down and passed around until everyone has a clear understanding and is in agreement.

Ground Rules

Many potentially deal-breaking problems can be avoided or reduced in scope by establishing a set of ground rules or norms that govern the ways in which people work together during the collaborative project. Ground rules might include the following:

- Criticize ideas and actions, not people.
- Respect differences in points of view and communication styles.
- Give everyone a chance to be heard.
- Demonstrate respect for others, even when you disagree.
- Respect other people's priorities.
- Do what you say you will do.

Once the rules have been established and agreed on, they can then be invoked as needed as the project progresses.

8

STRATEGIES FOR A SUCCESSFUL COLLABORATION

All men can see these tactics whereby I conquer, but what none can see is the strategy out of which victory is evolved.

—SUN TZU

There's no guarantee of success, no matter how careful your group's planning. Projects can be thrown off track, get bogged down, or simply fail to achieve anything of value, often for reasons beyond anyone's control, including sudden shifts in priorities or the economic climate. But there are some strategies that can increase the chances that your collaboration will achieve the worthwhile outcome that you and your colleagues are working for.

Keys to Successful Collaboration

Your collaborative efforts are more likely to be successful when you and your colleagues know how to do the following:

- Establish and maintain trust
- Keep the communication channels open
- Use conflict productively
- Maintain commitment
- Use brainstorming to generate high-quality ideas
- Get consensus on decisions

How to Establish and Maintain Trust

Have you ever watched a group of five-year-olds who don't know one another? They're usually a little wary. They want to know something about the other kids before they feel comfortable enough to play together. Are they friendly? Do they play gently, or roughly? Do they bite or steal toys? Trust doesn't come immediately; they need to get to know one another first.

People meeting for the first time in a collaborative group are likely to feel the same sort of wariness. Trust doesn't happen all at once. People need to know something about the other people's motives and to get a sense of what they are like before they can feel comfortable sharing information and ideas. They need to feel confident that the opinions and information they share will be kept within the group; to believe that their ideas, no matter how fanciful, will be treated with respect; and to know that they will be acknowledged for their contributions to a successful outcome. They need to know that the ideas of every member of the group will be valued equally, no matter what disparity there may be in experience, expertise, or position.

Establishing and maintaining trust must be a high priority at the beginning of any collaborative effort. This section explores some ways for the members of the group to do this.

Get to Know One Another

When we first interact with people we do not know, most of us instinctively hesitate to open up too much and share too much information—we're not sure how the other person will react, or how they might use anything we tell them. Getting to know one another is the first step in building enough confidence to feel comfortable sharing ideas and information freely. To do that, there is no substitute for face-to-face interaction. Even if group members are in far-flung locations, it's worth the investment of time and money to bring them together at the beginning of the project so they have a chance to put faces to names and learn a little about one another.

If it's not possible for people to meet in person, you can use video conferencing for introductory meetings so people can at least talk with one another face-to-face in real time. It's also a good idea to provide some opportunities in these early meetings for nonthreatening discussions or activities that involve everyone and demonstrate that everyone's ideas will be taken seriously.

Some ground rules can help the group avoid communication fatigue by ensuring that communication is convenient, accessible, and relevant. For example, the group can set up rules about how often to have meetings and how they will be run, along with guidelines that govern the type of information that will be distributed to everyone and the methods by which various kinds of information will be distributed.

Treat One Another with Respect

Conflict, even heated arguments, can be expected—indeed, encouraged—in any collaboration process. It's by sharing wildly different perspectives, ideas, and opinions that the group can come up with something entirely new. If there is no conflict, watch out: that's an indication that nobody really cares.

But conflict is productive only when members of the group focus their disagreements on the specific ideas and issues, not on the people voicing them. When people treat one another with respect, even when their ideas and perspectives differ significantly, everyone will feel more confident about participating freely in the process. If, on the other hand, people shoot down one another's ideas or, worse, offend them with their words, body language, or tone of voice, everyone is likely to shut down.

Really Listen to One Another

Trust comes when people feel confident that they will be listened to and heard. Group members need to listen attentively to one another, clarify as needed to make sure they understand, and respond in a way that shows that they have heard what the other person had to say. That kind of listening demonstrates that they are interested in and care about one another's ideas and opinions, even if they ultimately disagree.

Be Honest

Honesty creates trust. We trust other people when their behavior over time convinces us that we can count on them to be honest. Little destroys trust so quickly as behaving in an untrustworthy manner—lying, cheating, trying to cover over mistakes or deflect blame, taking credit for other people's ideas and so on. Even a single untrustworthy act can quickly result in distrust spreading throughout the group.

How much we trust others also depends on the degree of risk we have shared. There are two vital components to trust: engagement and letting go. A half-hearted commitment to actions does not inspire trust. When people hold back from engaging fully, they send a message that they may be undependable because their attention is divided. In collaboration this activated focus is so essential. Engagement creates energy for the group. Without it, collaborations go flat and creativity dries up, because creativity is all about risk engagement. In a less creative culture the status quo reigns, and the changes that are necessary for the trial-and-error process involved in collaboration are frowned on.

Booker T. Washington said, "Few things help an individual more than to place responsibility upon him, and to let him know that you trust him." After you place your trust in someone, though, you should try not to micromanage him. Attempting to manipulate the relationship by continuing to attach to outcomes or control of the situation prevents the other person from fully participating in the collaboration and inhibits your own performance. Such manipulation endangers the collaborative effort by disturbing the delicate interplay and dynamics of creativity and emergence (Farmer, 2009).

Honor Your Commitments

The members of a collaborative group need to be able to count on one another to do what they say they will do. Otherwise, either things won't get done or some people will end up shouldering the bulk of the work. Trust comes when people know that they can depend on one another to carry out the responsibilities they've agreed to. Trust and the group's morale can decline quickly if members miss deadlines, don't show up to meetings, or fail to provide essential resources.

Share the Blame When Things Go Wrong

An essential characteristic of a collaborative effort is that everyone involved shares the credit for a successful outcome. People are always glad to do that. But not every collaboration is successful, and even if the hoped-for outcome is eventually reached, there are liable to be missteps along the way. Groups have a higher level of trust when everyone is just as willing to share the blame when things go wrong as they are to share the credit when things go right.

Keeping the Communication Channels Open

If communication breaks down, the collaborative effort is unlikely to succeed. Even if the group is able to limp its way to some level of success, some or all of the group members may end up feeling dissatisfied with the process and the outcome.

This section details what a group should do to increase its ability to communicate and keep the communication channels open.

Establish Communication Protocols

When the group discusses its working process, the members need to answer questions such as these:

- How and how often should members communicate with one another?

- What should people communicate about?

- Which matters must be communicated to the entire group, and which to only certain members?

- What should—and should not—be communicated to people outside the group?

Discussing these kinds of questions before the work begins and then reviewing and revising the responses along the way will help your group avoid communication glitches that can end up snowballing into huge problems. Consider establishing clear protocols for the appropriate medium for each type of communication—face-to-face, electronic, telephonic, and so on.

Most groups use a combination of communication methods, of course. What's important is to figure out what works best in your particular situation so that people have access to project-related information, can share ideas and knowledge freely, and do not feel overwhelmed by the amount of information that goes back and forth during the course of the project.

Create Opportunities for Face-To-Face Interaction

These days we rely heavily on electronic communications, and for good reason—they allow us to communicate far more quickly and efficiently than in the past. We need to spend far less of our valuable time traveling to meetings when we have questions to ask, information to share, or something to discuss. Technology has made it possible for us to work with others to achieve highly complex goals without ever meeting them in person.

This dwindling of face-to-face interactions can be detrimental to the team spirit and pursuit of the common goal if the collaborative group does not give special attention to communication. The group must build in time and obtain the resources for face-to-face communication, both at the beginning of a project and throughout the process, especially when members are getting to know one another, when brainstorming ideas, and at those vital times when key issues must be discussed and important decisions made.

Face-to-face communication can be beneficial in both formal and more relaxed situations. Formal meetings, either in person or using an online platform, let group members check in with one another, reconfirm the goal, review their working process, ask questions, raise issues, and brainstorm solutions to any problems that have come up. Informal in-person get-togethers are invaluable for building relationships and sharing knowledge.

Avoid Meeting Fatigue

Although face-to-face meetings are an essential part of the process, no one joins a collaborative effort to attend an endless round of meetings. Every meeting should have a clear purpose and agenda, and presenters should prepare carefully so the time is used as wisely as possible. Begin each meeting by reviewing the shared goal, to remind people of what they are working toward and the progress you have made so they can see how far you all have come.

Give Constructive Feedback

The creative part of collaboration happens when the members of the group build on one another's ideas to come up with something altogether new. This requires taking the time to consider and discuss all the ideas that come up, as they come up, thus allowing the group to add value to those ideas and generate new ones. Feedback is part of that process— constructive feedback that focuses on the ideas, not on the person, and takes everyone's ideas seriously, even if they might seem at first to be off the wall. Sarcastic or negative comments block the flow of ideas as surely as a dam holds a river back from flowing to its destination, and without a free-flow of ideas, the collaboration is unlikely to come up with anything worthwhile.

Use "And" Instead of "But"

The little word "and" has a lot of power. When idea is met by "but," followed by all the reasons that it is unlikely to work, there is nowhere else to go. "But" negates whatever was previously stated. When an idea is met by "and," followed by the ideas that it generates, people can move forward.

For example, suppose you propose this idea to your group: "Maybe we can stay focused on our customers' perspectives more easily if we include some customers in our strategic planning sessions." A response like "*But* we don't want customers knowing our business" or "*But* we tried that a few years ago and it didn't work" shuts down the discussion. Conversely, if people say, "Great idea . . . *and* we could find a customer from each segment of our target audience," that builds on the original idea. Maybe, in the end, the group will decide that the idea is unworkable. Still, by using "and" instead of "but," they have at least opened the way to taking the discussion as far as it can go. And who knows? The path might lead to a strategy that no one has ever thought of before.

Put Things in Writing

A written record is essential during the collaboration process to make sure that the group captures ideas and decisions. Our memories are short and fleeting; a written record can be referred to whenever there is some confusion or misunderstanding, or simply used as a reminder: "What was the idea that Mark came up with at last week's meeting?" "What did we decide to do about . . . ?" "Who agreed to do the research on . . . ?"

As mentioned in the preceding chapter, the group needs to write down its goal, plan of action, and ground rules at the beginning of the project. As they move forward, they need to capture the ideas that people come up with, key points from discussions, actions they take, and decisions they make, along with issues that come up later and how they were handled. Documents that affect everyone should be easily accessible by every member of the group.

Be careful, however, to avoid inundating people with information that they do not need. It can be overwhelming to receive e-mail after e-mail, complete with attachments that need to be downloaded and reviewed. When too many of these come through, people may postpone opening them until they "have a few free moments"; this seems to never happen, and they end up missing something important.

Ground rules for written communication can help control the flow. For example, you might decide that certain information will be sent out only in summary form; if someone needs the full document, they can ask for it. The ground rules should also address how to handle confidential information that should not be accessible to everyone.

Using Conflict Productively

Conflict is a natural and expected part of collaboration. It's by exploring different points of view that you dive more deeply into the issues, develop the ideas that are most likely to achieve the outcome you seek, and ultimately gain greater commitment to your decisions. But conflict can have the opposite effect: instead of helping the group achieve its objectives, conflict can result in people locking into their positions and shutting down or even leaving the group altogether. According to some experts, the inability to resolve conflicts can present the most critical obstacle to effective collaboration (Abramson & Rosenthal, 1995).

It's important to allow—indeed, to encourage—some divergent ideas early in the project. If the conflict seems to be creating tension in the group or blocking the flow of new ideas, it can be helpful to refer back to the discussion you had when starting up the project about how to handle conflict. Remind everyone about the importance of respecting differing points of view and really listening to them. The group may not agree with what someone says, but their idea might spur a radically innovative idea from others in the group that would never before have been considered if not for the initial "bad" idea.

You are not going to agree on everything—and that's okay. You have already agreed on the big principles—the goal you share. You're not trying to reach agreement on every detail but to find a way to get the results you want.

Secretary of Treasury Tim Geithner did a good job explaining unproductive conflict to a group of business leaders in Northwest Arkansas. His point: we've got big problems and we can sometimes almost reach a solution, but then someone adds something we absolutely can't agree to as a rider to a bill (his example was a gun control rider to a financial solution). That fundamental insurmountable conflict must be removed for a time, and the focus needs to return to the areas in which we can and want to work together, such as a strong country, good education, good defense, and a solid economy. We need to focus on problems we can solve and leave the others alone until later.

When Conflict Gets in the Way

When conflict seems to be getting in the way of the group's progress or interfering with relationships, consider whether people are doing any of the following:

- Focusing on personalities and personal traits instead of on issues or ideas
- Arguing for positions, instead of focusing on ideas for achieving a result
- Shooting down one another's ideas
- Being judgmental
- Trying to control the direction of the discussion
- Talking instead of listening
- Focusing on trivial points
- Going off on tangents
- Pushing for a solution or decision before everyone's ideas have been heard

Keep the Focus on the Common Goal

In the heat of conflict, it can be easy for people to forget about the shared goal that is the reason for the collaboration. When conflict seems to be bogging the group down or having negative effects on relationships, bring the focus back to what you are all working together to achieve. For example, start every meeting with a recap of what you're trying to achieve and how your team's work will help you get there.

The team leader assumes a coach-like role when dealing with internal conflict within the group. If a conflict between team members is allowed to continue in a sports setting, it will be detrimental to the team as a whole and they will likely begin losing competitions. In the same manner, internal conflict is damaging to a business team. The focus and energy must be placed on making the collaboration a successful one.

Resolve Personal Conflicts Quickly and Privately

It's a beautiful thing when you're collaborating with someone who can practically complete your sentences. It's less beautiful when you must constantly smooth the ruffled feathers of participants who differ in their viewpoints, work styles, or attitudes. Some teams are riddled with such personal conflicts. Those teams are usually short-lived and accomplish little of value.

As a group, you need to agree to foster an environment that is tolerant of different ideas and opinions, but *not* tolerant of personal slights or drama-infused conflicts. Critiques should be kept to the ideas expressed and not the people behind them. Personal conflicts need to be resolved outside the group, or if the members can't work it out, both need to go.

Maintaining Commitment to the Project

Collaboration requires more than an initial enthusiasm about the common goal. It requires an ongoing commitment from everyone in the group. That commitment keeps people energized and involved even when the project bogs down or encounters difficult obstacles. Agreement on the shared goal, trust, free and open communication, and an effective conflict resolution process go a long way toward maintaining the initial commitment. Here are some other steps the group can take.

Clarify Roles and Responsibilities

To stay committed, people need to feel involved, useful, and valued throughout the collaboration process. That means making sure that every member of the group knows what he or she is supposed to do and how that effort contributes to achieving the goal. Because not everyone will be involved at every stage of the project, the group needs to pay special attention to keeping people in the communication loop and finding ways to engage the less active participants regularly.

Respect People's Other Priorities

The people who participate in collaborative projects usually have a lot on their plate. When setting priorities, the group needs to consider other responsibilities and projects that could impact members' commitment to the collaboration process and project deadlines. Members who have very little time or schedule flexibility should disclose this. The group may decide that the project requires too much time for that person to participate and can look for a different team member.

Recognize Accomplishments and Celebrate Milestones

Depending on the issue, a collaborative project might take anywhere from a few hours to a number of years. Thus it is important to keep everyone's head in the game through some occasional recognition of success. This does not have to be formal or costly, but should simply call attention to the fact that the group's commitment to the project has paid off in the short term and indicate that continued commitment will allow them to accomplish the final goal. The morale boost of, say, a group lunch can bring new energy to the project and inspire confidence as they begin working on their next milestone.

Using Brainstorming to Generate High-Quality Ideas

As mentioned in earlier chapters, brainstorming is a prime way in which groups come up with the truly innovative ideas and solutions that distinguish successful collaborations from less successful ones. The idea of brainstorming is to generate—and capture—as many ideas as possible and, if necessary, build on those ideas to come up with something new. Only after the group has drained the well, so to speak—by giving every member a chance to contribute and come up with what seems to be a significant number of ideas—do they step back to discuss and evaluate.

Here are a few guidelines for making the brainstorming process work:

- Start by making sure that everyone has the same understanding of the question you are trying to answer, the problem you are trying to solve, or the issue you are trying to address.

- Remind everyone of the ground rules: give everyone a chance to speak; listen to and respect one another's ideas; focus on the ideas, not the person; do not criticize or comment on any idea until all the ideas are on the table; share only what you are comfortable sharing; and so on.

- Use a facilitator to keep the group focused and a recorder to capture the ideas (these responsibilities can be rotated around the group).

Rules Help People Open Up

Rules for the brainstorming process can free people to participate fully. When I was a member of the Young Presidents Organization (YPO), we had Sharing Forums (small groups). Some high-level public figures opened up and shared somewhat confidential information, because the Forum was rules-based, and there was a system of principles in place. The rules made it a safe environment in which to share with the others in the group, and, just as with brainstorming, new ideas could be developed from ideas that were shared.

Tim Moore, one of the authors of "The Ideal Collaborative Team" (Ditkoff, Moore, Allen, & Pollard, 2005), describes the way in which Google uses brainstorming to encourage people to come up with innovative new ideas. "With a work force of 5,000 employees, dozens of projects are underway at Google at any one time. Roughly ten percent of employee work time is allocated to dreaming up blue-sky projects. Idea mailing lists circulate freely. Google encourages food fight–like *idea moshes*. Rule number one is 'no idea can be called *stupid* or *too wild*.' Brilliant arrogance is okay as long as someone's brashness doesn't break positive mood and momentum."

Getting Consensus on Decisions

You can't expect everyone to agree on everything, but attaining some level of consensus can help facilitate progress. Even animals and insects have innate ways to attain collective alignment. For example, bees use a complex system of consulting one another before choosing a hive, in a process that London scientists say could help humans make better decisions. Swarms send out groups of scout bees to assess the quality of a potential site. The insects then report back and do a "dance" to describe the location and benefits of the site. The swarm then comes to a group decision by revisiting the sites recommended by other bees until a consensus emerges and all the bees are performing the same dance (Gray, 2009).

The members of your collaborative group likely won't be literally dancing, but there is a certain metaphorical "dance" that is used as people select ideas and solutions that are most likely to move the group forward toward consensus.

Agree on What Kinds of Decisions Require Consensus

If you rush the decision-making process, some group members may not be fully committed to the decision, even if they might have agreed to it. Reaching consensus does take time, but consensus may not be necessary for every decision the group makes. Decide in advance which kinds of decisions must be made by consensus and which can be made by majority vote, or even by subgroups without the entire group's participation. Specialized subgroups may have all of the relevant knowledge and experience that is needed to make the call on routine issues anyway.

Make Sure Everyone Has the Same Understanding of the Decision

All too often, groups make decisions and then act on them without making sure that everyone understands them in the same way. That lack of common understanding can result in a lack of commitment and create serious problems down the road. So before a decision is implemented, it is important to write it down and check to be sure that everyone has the same understanding of what the group has agreed to do. In consensus, not everyone has to agree with the decision, but everyone has to be willing to abide by it. If there is any confusion or hesitation, take whatever time is needed to clarify and perhaps to revisit the decision before moving forward.

After the process is complete, it should be evaluated to identify possible next steps. The participants should look at their original written goals to determine what parts of the process worked well and what parts should have been done differently. They should be able to clearly identify whether they have accomplished their goals and whether there is a follow-on project that could be worthwhile. The conclusion could range from "mission accomplished" to the recommendation that the issue be approached with a team that has a completely different culture and perspective. All of the knowledge and information from the effort should be stored electronically, so that future efforts can leverage learnings and any technology methodologies that may have been built.

9

THE ROLE OF TECHNOLOGY AND SOCIAL MEDIA IN COLLABORATION

*Do you realize if it weren't for Edison we'd be
watching TV by candlelight?*

—AL BOLISKA, RADIO AND TV PERSONALITY

For many of today's companies, technology that enables and facilitates collaboration is a necessity. Global Vision International (GVI) is such a company. GVI sends more than 3,000 volunteers a year to work on more than 150 humanitarian and sustainability projects in 40 countries. Although the company maintains three central offices—one in the United States, one in the UK, and one in Australia—nearly all of its staff of three hundred people work remotely.

According to GVI Marketing Director Aaron Chan, technological tools are essential to the company's operations. "We rely on Skype and GoToMeeting to communicate as a team, share information, build on one another's ideas, discuss strategies, check in with one another . . . just about everything." GVI team members use Google Docs and Dropbox to store and share documents, share their calendars, and schedule meetings.

"Google Calendar is a great tool for us. It automatically adjusts times for different time zones, and it lets us see at a glance when people will or won't be online."

It wasn't so long ago when everyone had to be in the same building to share information and knowledge, brainstorm ideas, and develop strategies. However, the era when people working together on projects needed to be just down the hall from each other has clearly passed. Today's global economy makes it likely that our colleagues, customers, and others with whom we do business will be in widely scattered locations—and even in very different cultural settings.

Fortunately, modern technology makes it possible for collaboration to occur even among people who, like GVI staff members, are in vastly different locations and time zones. Today's technological tools allow us to communicate quickly and easily with one another, no matter where we are. We have countless options for exchanging information and ideas, holding meetings in real time, and working together on strategies, plans, and documents.

Obviously, including a section about collaboration-related technology almost guarantees that some of the content in this book will be outdated as soon as it rolls off the press; still, it would be irresponsible not to discuss the types of instruments that make real-time collaboration possible—as of this writing. Therefore, this is not a definitive guide to specific applications. Instead, please view the applications mentioned in this chapter as examples of the kinds of tools that you can use to further your collaborative efforts.

A Little History

During the last three decades of the twentieth century, personal computers brought about massive changes in the way people worked together. Intracompany communication was sped up, and teams discovered that they could collaborate more efficiently by using computers. More recently, due to the acceptance of software as a service (SaaS) and the power of cloud computing, collaborative tools are popping up in all varieties and becoming cheap and easy to use. At the time of this writing it is safe to say that many of the most popular tools reside at Google. Frankly, I don't even remember how people communicated prior to the use of Google Docs. Google continues to innovate as the company acquires, develops, and advances collaborative tools.

The mother of today's collaborative tools was based on the concept of a collaborative editor—a software application that allows several people to edit a computer file using different computers. There are two types of collaborative editing: real-time and non-real-time. Real-time collaborative editing (RTCE) is synchronous (simultaneous), meaning that users can edit the same file at the same time. Non-real-time collaborative editing is asynchronous, meaning that editors do not edit the same file at the same time (similar to revision control systems). Today's collaborative software generally permits both synchronous and asynchronous editing in any given instance. The first synchronous text editor was introduced in the late 1960s, although it took decades for actual implementations to hit the real world.

At first, simple computers that slowly ran customized software allowed employees within an office to work together on a problem or issue by giving everyone access to different parts of the project. This was a great step toward effective collaboration within a specific workplace, but it was severely limited—for example, someone who was working in London could not easily collaborate on a project with her colleagues in New York.

That changed in the 1980s, when the Internet and e-mail revolutionized the way we do business. E-mail, which emerged as the first major form of electronic communication, made it possible for team members to communicate quickly despite geographical separations. It was soon followed by huge improvements in conference calling and video conferencing that made remote interaction easier, cheaper, and more comfortable. E-mail made the collaboration process far more efficient, partly because the time and money needed for travel could be significantly reduced. Although these early tools were still relatively slow and cumbersome, the reduced need to consider location when putting together a team meant that collaborative teams could now comprise the most talented individuals, no matter where they lived and worked.

The technological innovations of the past two decades have given us a vast array of tools to improve the ways in which we collaborate. Now they are moving online into the "cloud," enabling members of a collaborative team to share documents and data far more rapidly and efficiently, without the need to purchase, install, and maintain compatible software. At the same time, another revolution seems to be taking place as a result of the increasing availability of social networking, which is proving to be a powerful tool for collaborators. In the coming decade, we can expect more in the way of business-oriented enterprise tools that leverage the power of social networking to foster business collaboration tools (Indinopulos, 2011).

The Collaborative Benefits of Cloud Computing

"Cloud computing" refers to the on-demand provision of resources (data, software) via a computer network, rather than from a local computer. To understand cloud computing, consider a public utility such as a water company. Centralized water companies freed individuals from the chore of pumping water for use in their homes and alleviated all of the tasks involved with digging and maintaining a well. Public water consumers were able to access the water they needed when they needed it. Similarly, cloud computing allows companies to trade the fixed costs of infrastructure and software for a pay-as-you-go system in which they only pay for what they need. Instead of IT being a huge capital expenditure, it becomes an operating expense. The upfront costs of cloud-based compared with the cost of in-house systems may not be vastly different, but factor in the indirect costs of personnel to run the in-house servers, space needed to house the servers, and the cost of extra electricity to cool them, and cloud computing becomes more attractive.

There has been a lot of excitement about the infrastructure of the cloud concept itself, but users are coming to realize that it isn't so much the cloud as an infrastructure that is so different, new, and exciting, but the empowerment that the cloud will enable. The cloud is accelerating the mainstream usage of collaborative technology tools, so that people can work with each other more efficiently and effectively. Users can submit a task, such as word processing, to the service provider without actually possessing the software or hardware. The user's computer, which serves as a basic display terminal connected to the Internet, may contain very little software or data. Because the cloud is the underlying delivery mechanism, cloud-based applications and services can support any type of software application or service in use today.

Mobility and Collaboration

With the power of mobility that has been put in everyone's hands in what we oddly still call a "cell phone," collaboration has become even quicker, more dynamic, and more energetic. Just as with the cloud, the excitement over the hardware will subside in time—it is the empowerment the cell phone brings that is revolutionary.

Mobility enables people to accelerate collaboration because it advances the speed of iteration. Iteration, which is critical to fast and furious collaboration, is the act of repeating a process, usually with the aim of approaching a desired goal or target or result. Iterations in a collaborative project context may refer to the technique of developing and delivering incremental components of business functionality, product development, or process design, as the results of each repetition are used as the starting point for the next iteration. A single iteration results in one or more bite-sized but complete packages of project work that can perform some tangible business function. Multiple iterations help create a fully integrated concept, idea, product, or service and lead to innovation.

The Collaborative Nature of Social Networking

The recent uprisings in the Middle East demonstrate how easy today's social media makes it for people to communicate with one another and organize themselves to achieve a goal. According to Ethan Zuckerman, in an article titled "The First Twitter Revolution?", Facebook, blogs,

YouTube, and other social media played an important role in toppling the Tunisian president, Zine el-Abidine Ben Ali. "It's likely," Zuckerman wrote, "that news of demonstrations in other parts of the country disseminated online helped others conclude that it was time to take to the streets" (Zuckerman, 2011).

The foundation of collaboration is communication and sharing. That's what social media is all about, and that's why collaborative online networks can be so powerful and efficient. The exact role of social media and technology in the recent uprisings has been debated, but it is indisputable that these tools accelerated and amplified voices that had been silenced for decades. The very tools that brought down leaders and forced the international community to intervene in Libya are now being used to challenge the status quo and shape the future. They bring empowerment through knowledge and the ability to assemble groups and distribute information more quickly. In fact, we'll never know how many similar revolutions might have occurred in the past had the technology existed to allow people to collaborate and leverage one another's ideas quickly.

The relevance of social networking for organizations is certain to grow: today's children, who will populate our future workforce, are especially adept at this new tool. Although some parents may view these as a distraction from their children's "real" education, social networking is here to stay, and the more successful we are at incorporating it into our lives now, the smoother the transition will be as today's children mature and enter the new innovative workplace of tomorrow.

Increasingly, the workforce will be made up of people who have grown up using technology and social media. Those who scarcely hesitate before sharing what older generations would have considered personal and private information with a wide circle of "friends"—many of whom they have never met—are unlikely to feel uncomfortable sharing what their elders would have considered proprietary or confidential information with their collaboration partners.

Information Overload or Filter Failure?

One of the main benefits of social technology—and of the Web in general—rests in its lack of structure—at least in our ability to surrender the concept of structure that we have long held dear. The Google founders were the first to figure this out in a meaningful way. They realized that packaging data into tidy digital folders was an unrealistic endeavor; too much information was already being created every second, and we would drive ourselves crazy trying to keep up. Just let all that data be, they said. Google will go back and find the most relevant information for you whenever you need it. The Web 2.0 era further advances searches with even more features, mainly tagging, to assist in making things findable in this unstructured world.

On the heels of Google came Facebook, Twitter, and the general emergence of activity streams. These fire hoses deliver an endless stream of unstructured data and information generated by both people and machines. Some of it may be annotated and tagged, but it is still lightweight in its organization. Lightweight technologies do not require a heavy up-front investment or operational requirements, and yet they usually still meet many management and strategic application requirements.

Enterprise social networks strive to return only the most relevant search results, as Google does. However, many people still complain of having too much data and information to process. In response, many consultants or social media experts will cite technology chronicler Clay Shirky: "It's not information overload, it's filter failure" (Shirky, 2008). The problem is, when it comes to using these tools inside companies to get work done, it's not filter failure that is worrisome; it's execution and prioritization failure within those filters. Filters have improved and are continually getting better. In fact, it's an area in which enterprise social networks are ahead of consumer social networks. In many enterprise social platforms, you can filter by group or virtually any object type, which helps put relevant information at your fingertips.

But although filtered enterprise social networking tools give people greater awareness of colleagues, projects, and initiatives in their company, it's harder to keep track of which things need doing first. When we collaborate on a significant number of work issues, we must ensure that individuals—and the groups they interact with—know where they stand on the tasks, projects, and issues involved. And this must be done without imposing too much structure, as business processes change quickly.

A Look at the Tools

E-mail is still the most widely used collaborative tool. Rarely will you find yourself working with someone who does not use e-mail regularly. And in almost every organization people are also using other popular types of collaboration and networking tools, such as the following:

• *File Sharing.* As mentioned earlier, collaborative editing software allowed early personal computer users to share the files they were working on, but the programs' capabilities were very limited. Users had to download documents, make changes, and then upload the revised document so that others could access them. Even today, many people still share files by e-mailing them back and forth, which takes time and can easily result in confusion over which version of a document is the most current. The confusion is now unnecessary. File sharing tools such as Google Docs, Syncplicity, Docs, SugarSync, and Dropbox let members of the team organize, store, manage, update, and access shared files. The online software handles the details. When someone makes changes, the files are automatically updated, so everyone has immediate access to the most recent version.

Social bookmarking (or social tagging) is not exactly sharing of the files themselves; rather, it is a reference to the resources that can be shared. It is a method for internet users to organize, store, manage, and search for bookmarks of resources online. Some popular bookmarking sites are CiteULike, Delicious, Google Reader, and StumbleUpon.

- *Blogs.* Blogs might not be the best choice for project-oriented collaboration, but they are great for sharing individual knowledge and experience, as well as for spurring discussion, which might be useful for brainstorming.

- *Wikis.* A wiki is a website that the users develop and maintain. Wikis are well suited to collaboration because any user can add and edit content, although a caretaker (or more than one) is usually assigned to make sure the information makes sense, is relevant to the topic, and is useful. Well-managed wikis remain dynamic and continually build on the existing knowledge base. Wikipedia is the best-known example of a wiki; some other popular wiki platforms are PBworks, Wetpaint, Wikia, Wikimedia, and Wikispaces. (In fact, this book's foreword was written by a group of forty collaborators after I popped up a wiki.)

- *Microblogging.* Microblogging services, such as Twitter, are useful for collaboration. They are better suited to whole-group interaction than individual instant messages, because information can be broadcast via microblog from one person to the whole group. Business-related microblogging applications such as Yammer can help employees stay connected by sharing Facebook-like status messages such as "I'll be on vacation next week" or "Friday's meeting will be at 1 P.M. instead of 3:30." It is important, however, to set up guidelines for the appropriate use of microblogs in your organization. They are clearly not the correct tools to use for complex discussions.

- *Forums.* Discussion forums, also known as message boards or bulletin boards, are among the oldest collaborative tools, and they are still very useful for sharing and discussing ideas. When using forums, group members should make sure the information they post on a particular thread is relevant to that particular topic. That not only keeps the forum as useful as possible but also makes it easier to search for previously posted information. Forums can be used throughout the collaborative process. Brainstorming and in-depth discussions or informal question-and-answer sessions can be accommodated on a group's forum.

- *Web-based meeting rooms.* Web-based conferencing services such as WebEx and GoToMeeting, which have sprung up during the past few years, offer collaborative groups an alternative when in-person meetings are not feasible. These services allow group members to meet in real time, no matter where they are located—all they need is an internet browser. The people participating in the meeting can hear—and sometimes see—one another, share documents, brainstorm, give each other feedback, ask questions, and do most of the other activities they would do in a face-to-face meeting. Meetings can also be recorded so that any group member who cannot attend can watch the proceedings later. Like face-to-face meetings, web-based meetings must be carefully planned to be useful.

- *Internet-based conference calling.* The line between web-based meetings and conference calls is becoming more blurry as conference calling becomes more advanced. The visual collaboration that occurs in many web-based meetings and with video conference calling enables face-to-face communication when collaborators cannot physically be in the same location. Increasingly, cell phones are being used not only for conference calls, but also for video conference calls, making collaborative communication more convenient than ever. As people become more familiar with the popular service providers, such as Skype, they are turning to them more often to conduct team projects (Byrne, 2010).

What Tools Do You Need?

Technological tools are like other tools in that before deciding which tool you want to use, you should figure out what you are trying to accomplish for your business. Just because something is being discussed in technology news does not mean it is applicable to the specific problem your company is trying to solve or improvement you are trying to make. Often the conversation begins with "We need a wiki." That may actually be the best solution, but it should be the result of a discussion. Begin instead by determining your goal from a business perspective, then decide which tool or set of tools are right for you. For example:

- *You want to build a knowledge base.* If you want to keep team members apprised of current developments in your industry field, you might use a wiki, to which employees contribute information. Be sure to assign a gatekeeper who will delete old information so that the team can stay up-to-date.

- *You want to encourage the sharing of innovative ideas.* Today's businesses must be able to get their new ideas to market at an ever-increasing pace. Blogs or forums can be useful for sharing, exploring, and improving upon ideas.

- *You want to be able to share information securely with team members outside your organization.* Collaboration often requires sharing of confidential or proprietary knowledge, documents, and information with customers and other collaboration partners who do not work for your organization. The use of web-based file-sharing allows you to do that in a secure, auditable way.

- *You want team members to stay in touch.* Microblogging is a simple and quick way for people to keep up with one another between meetings and for quick updates.

- *You want people to stay connected on a personal level.* Social networking tools such as Facebook, which people may well be using anyway, can help people build and maintain relationships by staying connected at a personal level, even when they can't meet around a water cooler.

Issues to Consider

As mentioned earlier in this book, an organization's leadership may be reluctant to let employees use many of the technological tools that facilitate collaboration. Managers generally have concerns about wasted time and sharing of confidential information. They range from the simple— "Do we allow Facebook access at work, risking the downside of wasting time versus the upside of increased collaboration and more rapid communication and research?"—to the complex—"Do I open up a wiki for employees, customers, vendors to share ideas when we are not used to letting anyone, even executives, share information about our people, our processes, and our technology?"

These are valid issues. But it's a balancing act, and when thinking about which tools you don't want to allow employees to use or what restrictions you want to place on the use of certain tools, also consider the opportunities that you might miss if your employees are not able to collaborate effectively with others both inside and outside the organization. The advantages are probably greater than the disadvantages in most cases.

Collaboration at GE

GE offers an excellent illustration of how technology can be used to enable collaboration. Well known for its research and innovation, which requires immense efforts of collaboration mainly because much of the research is multidisciplinary, GE brings researchers from all fields together to work toward a common goal. GE has over thirty-six thousand technologists working in their Global Research Centers and the Energy, Technology Infrastructure, GE Capital, and Home & Business divisions. The collaborative efforts become even more challenging due to the cross-national and cross-cultural collaboration required for the latest technologies that GE develops.

Recognizing the importance of collaboration, GE has designed its workforce so that researchers across divisions and in different centers can communicate about and contribute ideas to different projects. For example, the GE Energy division uses various tools to ensure that collaboration is smooth at all levels.

One of these, called "ProjectNet," is housed on the company website; it provides a secure platform for communication and workflow between GE, customers, and suppliers worldwide. This platform can be used to execute all phases of a project, from inquiry through plant development, sale, design, construction, commissioning, and operation. Available in six languages, ProjectNet can be accessed from anywhere in the world, at any time, by a user with an internet browser and valid user ID and password.

ProjectNet gives people greater flexibility and helps them collaborate beyond the boundaries that companies traditionally impose, while ensuring that documents get sent to the correct places regardless of where they are generated. It is an example of a company-specific application that goes much further than any off-the-shelf product. As a result, it offers greater depth and lots of possibilities. As collaborative sites are opened, GE offers courses to train proposal teams and customers on the use of ProjectNet (GE Energy, n.d.).

The Mayo Clinic

Another highly collaborative organization that makes use of many technological tools is the Mayo Clinic, which uses videoconferencing and web conferencing to extend—rather than to create—an already collaborative culture. Its Design Research Studio, formerly the SPARC Innovation Program, is widely recognized as the first design-based research and development laboratory for health services (Center for Innovation, n.d.).

The brainchild of Drs. Nicholas F. LaRusso, chair of the Mayo Clinic Department of Medicine, and Michael D. Brennan, associate chair of the department, the idea of SPARC began on a run. The central concept was a design studio embedded in a clinical practice, placing designers, business strategists, and medical professionals in close proximity to permit collaborations on a variety of projects. Its methodology, See-Plan-Act-Refine-Communicate, is a description of a design methodology that is rooted in the techniques of ethnography, prototyping, design thinking, and business integration.

Collaboration and Organizational Culture

For collaboration to be successful, the correct mind-set must be ingrained in the culture of the organization. When that innovative culture combines with the technological tools of today, the results can be staggering. The use of the tools alone does not guarantee that every undertaking will have a groundbreaking outcome, but learning to use new technology can make you better able to adapt to the even newer technology next year, next month, or tomorrow.

For firms to leverage these new technologies, however, some cultural shift is usually needed. Shifting a corporate culture that includes the deep psychology, attitudes, experiences, and beliefs of an organization is no easy task. That's what we will discuss in the final chapter of the book.

10

FOSTERING A COLLABORATIVE CULTURE IN YOUR ORGANIZATION

Culture eats strategy for breakfast.

—PETER DRUCKER

A corporate culture that embraces collaboration is the cornerstone for success in today's business environment. It is through collaboration that your business can maximize the talents of your associates, direct your team's energy, and initiate innovation. The right collaborative environment can make it possible to unleash everyone's potential to create exponential organizational growth. You'll benefit from superior-quality projects, more efficient teams, healthier staff dynamics, and an empowered proactive organization. It's what enables a company to achieve what James Collins and Jerry Porras describe as Big Hairy Audacious Goals (BHAGs) in their article "Building Your Company's Vision" (Collins & Porras, 1996). A BHAG encourages companies to define visionary goals that are more strategic and emotionally compelling. Those aren't easily achieved without a strong collaborative culture.

Evan Rosen, author of *The Culture of Collaboration*, couldn't have summed up the alternative any better when he said, "What paralyzes an organization is when management compromises value by failing to tap ideas, expertise and assets. What also paralyzes an organization is when requests for decisions languish in in-boxes rather than hashing out issues spontaneously. Paying a few people to think and paying everybody else to carry out orders creates far less value than breaking down barriers among silos and enabling people to engage each other spontaneously." In surveys you'll often find the concept of a collaborative culture as a top measure of what qualifies a company as one of the best places to work for recent grads; people want to make a difference, and collaborative companies give them the opportunity. In one recent survey of Best Places to Work, a senior financial analyst respondent said, "It was extremely important for me to join a company where I was challenged and inspired not only by the work, but also by the people around me. At Capital One, being smart, driven and collaborative is not reserved for the best-of-the-best; it's the status quo" (MacKenzie, 2011). According to various company releases, Capital One goes out of its way to stress its complex adaptive systems and virtual team collaboration, its spirit of collaboration, and its work with nonprofits, businesses, and government organizations. During the difficult economic times following the 2008 market crash, the company's culture allowed it to make some quick strategic decisions that may very well have saved it while other banks failed. It jettisoned its once-significant mortgage platform, GreenPoint Mortgage, and now Capital One ranks in the top quartile in its sector for long-term growth. Its culture has led to decisions that have helped it get through tough times and see its market capitalization more than double over the past two years.

Another example of the benefits of a collaborative culture comes from a company whose services are now so ubiquitous that we use them without even thinking of the company: Google. Google may well be the poster child for its collaborative culture. Recognizing that its most valuable asset is its employees' passions, Google encourages employees to form ad hoc "grouplets" to explore their ideas freely. The company claims that 50 percent of their products, including Gmail, are a result of the 20 percent of the time they encourage employees to use working with others on a product they are all interested in. Several grouplet organizers meet once a week to make sure these self-directed groups are not unintentionally working at cross-purposes with the company's interests (Mediratta & Bick, 2007).

Even if you realize that increasing collaboration within your organization would be beneficial, actually fostering a more collaborative culture can be challenging. Getting employees who are scattered around the country or even around the world to work closely with one another means establishing trust and keeping the lines of communication open. Younger members of the workforce may not have as much difficulty with trusting people they know only virtually and with communicating openly, because they are so accustomed to using social networking tools in their personal lives. However, some senior executives and managers may not see the value of information sharing. But if the company is to remain relevant in the emerging knowledge economy, those skeptical attitudes will have to change. No matter how long they've been in the workforce, many employees are likely to resist change unless they have a clear understanding of how a collaborative culture will be beneficial to them and the organization. Let's take a look at how to go about achieving this.

First Things First: Leadership

The driving force behind a collaborative culture is supportive leadership. For collaboration to work, everyone, from the CEO down, must be fully on board. Unfortunately, a company's management can have many reasons for not championing a collaborative effort. In most cases, the primary reason for discounting collaborative opportunities is that the return on investment (ROI) is sometimes ambiguous. Management easily grasps the idea that collaboration will require time, effort, and investment, but it doesn't always easily distinguish the return from those investments. For the organization's leadership to promote and support the necessary changes required to transform the organization, they need to understand the ways in which collaboration can positively affect the bottom line.

Vendors of collaboration services usually claim that their tools somehow improve business productivity. Sometimes these claims are straightforward, such as the proposition that videoconferencing or GoToMeeting services will reduce the need for costly travel. Other times, though, it isn't as easy to prove the business case for investment.

The consulting firm Frost and Sullivan recently published a white paper that addresses the challenge. According to the white paper, "This study is the first global study to determine a model for measuring return on collaboration (ROC). It provides clear evidence demonstrating a continuum of collaboration-driven performance, such that the deployment and usage of progressively more advanced IP-enabled collaboration technology yields increasing levels of organizational performance" (Frost & Sullivan, n.d., p. 1). Unlike a traditional ROI calculation, which tracks the amount of contribution directly received from the amount of money invested, ROC captures the broader concept of improvement that results from collaboration being used in specific functional areas, relative to the overall amount of money invested.

The study included important measures that spanned various key performance areas including overall customer satisfaction, sales and profit growth, labor productivity, and innovation (that is, the opportunities for future economic benefit). Companies that used collaborative principles exhibited 72 percent better performance, with the most significant consequences including innovation, sales growth, and profit growth. In other words, the functional areas that leveraged collaboration benefited a lot more than the typical ROI calculation would have implied when a broader measure was considered. As an example, a typical ROI calculation for a decision about upgrading a corporate business continuity platform will usually consider the costs of potential downtime if the old system has failed, but it may miss some potential upsides of the investment. For instance, that upgrade might enable the sales group to sell more using the stronger platform in its discussion with clients, the IT group may benefit from additional flexibility offered by the new system, or human resources turnover may be reduced because users enjoy the efficiency of a stronger platform. Simple ROI calculations may overlook some of the returns like these that should have been incorporated in the "R" in ROI.

As we all know, though, there are many beliefs and values that run much deeper than how we calculate the benefits of investments. Leaders whose experience is deeply rooted in a competitive, secretive culture or a rigidly hierarchical corporate structure may also be skeptical of the benefits of sharing information freely. They may have an inclination against allowing employees the freedom to work with each other to explore and develop ideas on their own. To be supportive, management must believe and trust that employees can accomplish more by working collaboratively than by working individually. In many cases, they must recognize the need for drastic hierarchy design changes to make their organization more conducive to collaboration and help the collaborative culture take root by continually demonstrating that commitment.

Managers at all levels must lead by example and internalize the goal of becoming more innovative through collaboration. They must demonstrate that they are willing and eager to hear ideas from all team members at every level of the organization and follow through by implementing the ones that work. They have to hold all employees accountable for implementing changes in their daily routines and adopting new collaborative procedures, tools, and strategies.

Paying close attention, especially in the early stages of the shift to a collaborative environment, allows management to address concerns, real or perceived, about any shortcomings or failures in any of the new processes or tools. Of course, every collaborative effort will not yield optimal results, but every effort can be a learning experience. Identifying, correcting, and being accountable for problems as soon as they come to light will give employees more confidence in management's decision to modify the organizational strategy. Team members will be more apt to try something new when they know they will not be stuck with it if it does not work as planned.

Let's consider an example of a company that has successfully fostered greater collaboration.

BP's Peer Assist Program

BP, formerly known as British Petroleum, might have recently lost its way, but it is a good example of a company that was once stuck in the mud and then transformed its culture to generate huge profitability and significant economic value. If we step back in time, we can see its leader-driven make-over and the results. In the late 1980s, BP was a politicized, top-heavy bureaucracy managed through a cumbersome matrix structure. Performance was declining, the company was heavily indebted, and by 1992, the company faced a financial crisis that almost resulted in bankruptcy.

After Lord John Browne became BP's CEO in 1995, he implemented a peer assist program designed to enable entrepreneurial thinking across the company, which became part of the culture. The underlying philosophy is that performance is increased when executives and managers actively learn from collaborating with one another. Each peer group includes multiple business units, which in many organizations would be naturally competitive. At BP, the multiple business units in the peer group are responsible to each other as well as to their internal group—even to the point of peer group bonus attainment. The program drove innovation through collaboration and resulted in reductions in the cost of field development and even extended the productive life of assets. Some of the unique leadership-driven attributes that created a collaborative culture were a stated goal of transferring knowledge instead of judging work, allowing teams to select their own reviewers who could help improve their performance, and engaging in peer problem-solving work sessions. In the years prior to Lord Browne's 2007 retirement, BP was successful and was rewarded with a stock price that tripled. BP used collaboration to improve its profitability and it worked. Its more recent failures, notably the 2010 Gulf Oil spill, suggest that the company might consider dusting off its old collaborative playbook to encourage innovation in the field of safety (Roberts, 2005).

Plan Carefully and Be Patient

It is human nature to resist change, even when we know the change will ultimately be beneficial. We may keep on smoking and eating double cheeseburgers with fries, even though we know that smoking and obesity can lower our quality of life or even kill us. Many people hold onto jobs they loathe simply because it's too difficult or seems too daunting to try something new. In many organizations, we keep following the same inefficient procedures year after year because they are getting the job done, if only just barely. This attitude of "If it isn't broken, don't fix it" keeps management from trying to go beyond the status quo to consider the possibilities of the progressive, more efficient, collaborative ways of doing things, even when the benefits are apparent.

Keep in mind that traditional corporate cultures do not become collaborative cultures overnight. You must give careful consideration to how to go about making the necessary changes and getting everyone on board. Changes must be explained, new procedures and processes must be described, and systems must be in place to support the new methodologies. Engage all of the employees in the process of figuring out how to make collaboration work well for your particular organization. The team members will be less resistant to change if it is instituted over time with clearly described rationale and benefits. When people are involved in discussions throughout the process, they are much more likely to embrace new initiatives.

All employees—at all levels of the organization, not just the executives—must be willing to participate fully in the transformation from a traditional to a collaborative environment. They must be willing to trade old familiar habits for new, more efficient ones if real success from collaboration is to be achieved. To achieve that level of participation, the leaders of the collaborative charge must focus on the principle of "What's in it for me?", so that everyone in the organization realizes that increasing collaboration will not only be advantageous to the culture of the organization but also help them as individuals. For example, if collaborating with the sales group will make the marketing group's point-of-purchase materials more effective, the marketing people will more quickly jump on the collaboration bandwagon.

Management must be disciplined enough to continue emphasizing the benefits until everyone is acclimated to the new culture and people are experiencing the benefits of the changes firsthand. Even if there isn't much resistance, this may take a while, because some people do not learn as quickly as others. However, in the long run, the increased efficiency across the organization will be worth the effort of the initial hand-holding to make sure the team members adopt the change. Of course, compliance will have to be monitored routinely.

Best Practices

There is no one recipe for creating and maintaining the perfect collaborative culture. Still, there are certain practices often found among organizations that are able to reap the benefits of that culture. These practices include the following:

- Establish trust
- Give people enough time to collaborate
- Provide access to people and information
- Encourage communication
- Help people hold productive meetings
- Provide tools that facilitate collaboration
- Develop a tracking system
- Provide training
- Hire for collaboration
- Recognize and reward collaborative efforts
- Nurture the collaborative environment forever

Establish Trust

The importance of trust to a collaborative project within a company cannot be overemphasized. Trust is vital to developing and maintaining a collaborative organizational culture. Employees have to be able to trust their leaders to act in the organization's best interest and do what they say they will do, which means that management must model the new behaviors and reward—not question—collaborative behaviors. Team members also need to trust that both management and their colleagues will be open with them, share information, respect them, and give them credit for their ideas. Without trust, not only will a collaborative environment fail to take hold, but people are likely to feel frustrated and angered by the failed attempt.

Because it is so much easier for people to trust one another when they *know* one another, it's important to create opportunities for people to meet face-to-face by providing the financial and time resources needed for people to travel to some conferences and meetings; the payoff to your organization will be well worth the costs. Make resources available for meetings and brainstorming sessions where people can get to know one another, learn about the experiences and expertise of other team members, and share valuable information.

Let's emphasize here that boondoggles are unwelcome. If you engage in too many offsite meetings, they will lose their effectiveness; indeed, they will be a waste of money and time. Repetitive team-building exercises that deliver few lasting benefits, executive PowerPoint parades that present numbers and graphs in majestic style but with no real substance— these are not necessary to maintain a collaborative culture. Ask people a month later what they remember from those meetings; they'll probably think first of the buffet. Meetings and other events designed to get people together need a valid reason, so that people involved feel that their time is being used wisely, and people outside are able to see the event as having been productive.

Give People Enough Time to Collaborate

Everyone is rushed these days. But reaping the benefits of collaboration takes time, and team members will often forgo opportunities to collaborate if they feel pressured to meet a deadline. Even when they know that collaborating would yield a better finished product, time constraints may tempt them to shoot for "good enough."

Even before Google and Hewlett-Packard started giving people time to invest in special projects, 3M was offering associates time off to explore their own innovations—resulting in many of 3M's most successful products to date. For example, in 1974 3M engineer Art Fry came up with a crafty invention. He thought if he could apply another colleague's adhesive to the back of a piece of paper, he could create the perfect bookmark. We now know it as the Post-it Note. Fry was able to come up with the iconic product as part of the "15 percent time" program at 3M. The program encourages employees to use a portion of their paid time to collaborate and innovate. This may seem like a soft employee benefit, but it has created significant economic value, and it has been mimicked by other technology oriented companies. Due to their plainness, Post-its seem as old-fashioned as the stapler and the hole-punch, but in many ways they are a consummate product of their time that is still sitting on desks in offices everywhere. In some ways, Post-its almost foreshadowed email as an informal, asynchronous form of communication—an easy way to link one piece of information to another in a contextual way. More important, many of the nearly twenty-three thousand patents at 3M came from the 15 percent program. It is a big part of their culture (Goetz, 2011).

Unfortunately, time constraints in today's workplace sometimes make it difficult, if not impossible, for people to collaborate effectively on a project. However, if you want employees to maximize their collaboration with colleagues, you may need to make adjustments in their schedules to enable them to get together as a team to brainstorm and generate and discuss ideas.

Provide Access to People and Information

Suppose you were an attorney hired to defend a crime suspect in court, but you were not allowed to see any of the relevant documents or interview any of the people who were involved in the case. How successful do you think you would be? Without that access, you would have a lot of trouble mounting an effective defense.

It's the same with collaboration—it's pretty hard to solve problems or address issues if you don't have access to the relevant people or information. To collaborate effectively, employees need access—and not just to information. Yet that access is often blocked because of preconceived notions that certain information is only for select people. Sometimes there is no explanation other than "It's just always been that way." For collaboration to succeed and a collaborative culture reach its full potential, that archaic attitude has to change.

Encourage Open Communication

The tendency of people in traditional organizations to protect or hoard information and resist sharing their ideas for fear that they will be ridiculed or someone else will take credit is a quick collaboration-killer. It's understandable: in too many organizations, people are questioned, not rewarded, for the very actions that are required for collaboration to succeed, and when people are operating in a purely competitive mode, they may be tempted to take credit for other people's ideas. However, collaboration requires an atmosphere of trust in which people feel free to communicate openly and often. They need to really listen to one another and respect ideas, even when they do not agree; share information without feeling that they are betraying "secrets"; and take the risk of introducing outside-the-box ideas that can lead to truly innovative solutions.

Help People Hold Productive Meetings

Collaboration may require quite a few meetings—because team members often need some face time to brainstorm ideas, iterate to innovate and build on each other's ideas, discuss alternatives, make decisions, come up with action plans, track their progress, and evaluate their results. To use that time productively and realize the full benefits of the collaborative process, meetings must have a clear purpose and be planned carefully.

Even short meetings should have an agenda. A detailed agenda demonstrates respect for the attendees' time and increases the chances of their
active participation. An agenda should include the following:

- Meeting objectives
- Action item review
- Specific topics you'll cover
- Any new action items

Participants should receive the agenda in advance of the meeting,
along with key information about the meeting, including time, place, and
what they need to bring. To help ensure that the meeting goes smoothly,
set up some up some ground rules for behavior, discuss what to do if discussions get off track, and decide on a decision-making process.

Effective meetings do not always have to be held off site to remove
the team members from potential interruptions and distractions. The
idea that you can get away from distractions at an offsite hunting lodge,
while skiing in Aspen, or at a convention in Las Vegas is not borne out in
reality. Often, the place *becomes* the distraction. Sometimes a team can
stimulate the best ideas by holding meetings in a place related to the
topic of their collaboration; for example, if they are working on improvements to inventory systems, that place may be the warehouse; if the topic
is related to the operations of a retail store, they might meet in the back
room of the store; if they are trying to come up with innovative solutions
for emergency room staffing problems, they could meet in a hospital; or
if they want to improve customer service, meet at customer locations.

In an effective meeting, participants do not just skip around from
thought to thought. Instead, they keep iterating to innovate and build on
each other's ideas. In a collaborative culture the intention is to continue
this process until the solution is found. To keep pushing those building
blocks ever higher, it is important that the communication flows freely.
Collegiality—the relationship between colleagues—is a cultural element

that can help open that flow during meetings. Associates will be more likely to work together in pursuit of a goal if they have a healthy rapport. Consider how little the U.S. Congress accomplishes during sessions where empathy wanes and how much they accomplish during periods of bipartisan civility and collaboration.

Provide Tools That Facilitate Collaboration

The vast array of technological tools available today make it easy for people to work together, stay in touch with one another, and monitor their progress while collaborating on a project. Unfortunately, companies that do not espouse a collaborative culture may not allow people to use those tools. If the organization is rigidly hierarchical, for example, a team member might avoid requesting a $9.99 download that will facilitate progress just to avoid a potential grilling from their boss or the accounting department. People are hesitant to download software to their laptops if the IT people deter it. If accessing Twitter or YouTube on company time is considered laughable or unprofessional, they likely won't be used even when they have business applications. Some companies discourage or even inadvertently deter usage of Skype, web meeting software, or groupware; some prohibit the use of discussion forums such as those available on Facebook or LinkedIn. Even when employees are allowed to use instant messaging and wikis, how many of them even know how to set up and use these tools?

Yet if you want to promote, encourage, and facilitate collaboration, you need to not only give people access to those tools (as discussed in Chapter Nine) but also provide training to ensure that they can use them correctly to maximize their effectiveness for your organization. We are *not* advocating that office hours be frivolously used for personal social networking. Our point is that these new tools must be readily accessible when there is *a business case* that they create economic value. The concept isn't exactly new; even office phones can be abused, but you wouldn't take them off everyone's desks because they might sometimes be used by some people in frivolous ways. Instead, you would manage their usage.

Develop a Tracking System

When ideas fly fast and furiously, knowledge can quickly disappear into the stratosphere. If you are truly interested in making the best use of collaboration, you need to develop a system and a process for capturing those ideas along with the decisions people make and the actions they take as a result of collaborative efforts. After all, an idea that turned out not to work in a certain situation might be perfect for another, and an action that turned out not to achieve the desired outcome can serve as a learning opportunity.

A knowledge management system can take many forms. Each organization should consider what is suitable. For example, document-based systems work well when the technology permits the creation, management, and sharing of formatted documents. Taxonomy-based systems are useful when there are terminologies that are often used to summarize ideas in documents. Systems based on artificial intelligence require greater complexity and customization, but they can be powerful in situations with very customized methodologies. Increasingly, social computing tools are making once-intimidating concepts in knowledge management much more accessible. For example, in a matter of minutes, at zero cost, a team can pop up a secure wiki that can help capture and share knowledge.

Provide Training

People may need training to function effectively in the new collaborative environment. Employees may need to develop or hone the key team-building skills—such as active listening, interpersonal communication, giving and receiving feedback, brainstorming, and decision making—that are essential for effective collaboration. The better their skills, the more comfortable they will feel with the collaborative process and the more successful their collaborations are likely to be.

Providing cross-training opportunities can also help to foster a collaborative environment. A collaborative culture requires knowledge sharing across the whole organization, not just within individual departments. Cross-training helps people in the organization not only get to know one another but also gain insight into how other departments work and how their work contributes to the organization's success.

Mix it up a little. Moving people around and having them learn other roles will make them more effective in their own duties. Gaining a better understanding of how all the departments work together to accomplish companywide goals will help eliminate silos and interdepartmental power struggles that can stifle collaboration. When people begin to see the big picture and view the departments as team members and the company as the team, the internal competition (for example, marketing versus accounting, sales versus operations, finance versus customer service) should subside as everyone works together to achieve success.

Hire for Collaboration

In Chapter Five we discussed the fact that some people are better at collaboration than others. To improve the collaborative environment in the organization, look for that kind of person when you hire. Design an interview process that helps you determine how well people will be able to work with others and participate actively in the collaboration process. Research has shown that managers have a tendency to recruit candidates in their own image, even when they are trying to be objective; if you want collaborative people to be hired, put collaborative people in charge of hiring.

Goldman Sachs offers an example of a hiring process that optimizes the chances of hiring people with the qualities the organization values. Their candidates sometimes interview with as many as sixty senior members of the firm—they say that just a single rejection can scuttle an interviewee's candidacy. This hiring process goes far beyond simply reviewing a résumé; they are looking for people with talent, drive, and ambition who are willing to work with the team. As a result, their new hires already have relationships with some of the partners and a sense of belonging that comes from knowing that they were chosen after a rigorous, highly selective interview process.

An effective hiring process that results in new employees who have the skills and characteristics needed for collaboration is just the beginning.

You need to think about what happens after someone is hired: Do people just get dropped into a team, or is there a real onboarding process? The first few weeks are critical—the new person is picking up cues about the company's culture from other employees' dress, their behavior, and what they talk about—or don't talk about. The onboarding procedures should emphasize the value of collaboration and establish new employees in networks that exude collaborative spirit.

Nokia provides another example. They are known for introducing new employees to at least a dozen team members, half from their own team, the rest from cross-boundary teams. As a result, within two weeks new hires are already are familiar with at least twelve people and multiple functions; more important, they understand that it is more than OK to talk to people outside their function. This is very different from what often happens in traditional organizations, where people may not even know the names of colleagues who work in cubicles that are three feet away and may have little communication except through e-mail.

Recognize and Reward Collaborative Efforts

There's a good reason why people post certificates on their walls and trophies on living room shelves. We all like to feel recognized for our accomplishments. An important part of the effort to transform a traditional organizational culture into a collaborative culture is coming up with ways to recognize and reward individuals and groups for their collaborative efforts. In the right atmosphere, individuals are more likely to champion an idea and take ownership of a project or task right up front. For example, you can incorporate collaboration into performance reviews, make resources available for rewards and celebrations of success, and provide opportunities for peer recognition. If a project sponsor bases performance incentives on collaboration and the result is successful, the depth of the leaders' and team members' participation will become stronger.

Assessing the performance of an individual in a collaborative environment may require a new appraisal system that incorporates peer feedback from other team members. In that case, organizations may need to modify the performance appraisal systems currently in place and adjust their cultural ideas about employee evaluations (Sinclair, 2011).

Nurture the Collaborative Environment Forever

Maintaining a collaborative culture is often more challenging that just creating one, but that's where all the value is. Corporate histories are littered with instances of a hard-won collaborative culture dying a slow death through either apathy, changes in leadership, or loss of momentum. For example, Ocean Spray, an organization with deep roots in collaborative principles, came to realize that its culture needed a shot in the arm. The company has a very collaborative history—it was started in 1930 as a co-op of three cranberry growers with the common goal of expanding their market. In recent years, senior management realized that there was potential benefit from improving collaboration not only with external groups but also within the organization, particularly among the different age groups that make up their employee base. The younger employees thought the more senior team members weren't listening to them, and the baby boomers thought the newer team members only valued their positions in the company but contributed little. The executives remedied the tension by having the different groups work together collaboratively. As the groups gained a better understanding of each other, they gained more respect and realized the value each added to the organization.

By recognizing the need to have employees interact with other employees with whom they were not inclined to communicate, Ocean Spray obviously figured out how collaboration could improve its bottom line and boost its ROI. In a September 15, 2010 interview, Ocean Spray's CEO, Randy Papadellis, reported that despite the rough economy, the company had just experienced its most successful year ever (Papadellis, 2010).

Once everyone in the organization has embraced the collaborative culture, benefits such as time savings from eliminating redundancies will become apparent. When people work together effectively, they will be able to more easily handle the sudden changes of today's global economy and take on unexpected projects that require rapid implementation.

However, just as fruit trees do not continue to thrive and bear fruit without watering and pruning, a collaborative culture also will not thrive without ongoing attention. Once the necessary behavior and attitude changes have taken place and the essential processes, systems, and procedures have been adopted and placed into operation, you must continue to nurture the initiative. And it's important to note that if collaboration attempts fail once or twice, the process should not be abandoned or employees returned to operating within insular business units. The culture must be fully supportive of the process even if not all projects yield the desired results. The process of collaboration takes time and energy, and not all efforts will produce successful results.

In summary, each organization has an opportunity to define, develop, and nurture its own collaborative culture. It isn't always completely formulaic, but it definitely involves empowering collaborative champions to create the right environment, supporting collaborative people, leaders, tools, and technology that drive results. In addition, the team cannot lose sight of the fact that defining any culture takes time, experimentation is necessary, and changes are OK.

It takes considerable time to build and maintain a collaborative environment that becomes integrated in the organization's DNA, but as everyone gets acclimated, this culture becomes more instinctual. It will soon become apparent that helping each other work through issues together will enable the whole team to create value and realize success in their endeavors.

Changes are happening quickly. CEOs and emerging leaders in all sorts of organizations are realizing that collaboration is paradoxically the most competitive weapon in their arsenals. As the culture of collaboration grows ever stronger in the global economy and in the world as a whole, it becomes even more critical that organizations modify their own business processes and environments to keep up. With the advice and examples you take away from this book, you are ready to help your organization take those essential steps.

AFTERWORD

If I have seen further it is by standing on the shoulders of giants.

—ISAAC NEWTON

This revolutionary shift from the traditional way of doing things to collaboration is unstoppable. An entire generation has now grown up with the idea that sharing is good, and they are comfortable with the technology that enables it. There is a cultural shift to sharing instead of protecting and hoarding information, knowledge, and expertise, and the advantage is increasingly going to the people who know how to share. There are win-win opportunities for individuals and organizations willing to open up and trust one another.

And we need to do this now. The urgent problems facing us in our increasingly complex and global world will not go away by themselves, and they will not be solved by the old way of doing things. We need to change the game. It won't be easy. But it's well worth the effort.

The foreword was the most satisfying part of this book. I asked a group of people to collaborate on it, and they came up with quality content that I never could have imagined by myself. It was much better than anything I could create alone. Along with that, it also included a lot of kind words that are much more than I deserve. I can't thank everyone enough for their contributions. Toward the end of the process, I explained my book writing experiences with Bob, one of the cocollaborators on the foreword. I described how difficult it was to try to really convey the message the way I had imagined; I have to believe no author ever feels like he's done his ideas justice. I am clearly no exception.

I also explained how impressed I was by the robust participation in writing the foreword. The book's foreword was written as a collaborative exercise—meaning that everyone who collaborated did the work for me. Even for an ardent champion of the practice of collaboration, I was amazed at how well the process really does work! If the group is motivated and talented, it will wallop anything a single individual can accomplish.

Bob made a lighthearted but insightful comment: "There's your epilogue: next time everyone else should just collaborate on the *whole* book."

REFERENCES

Abramson, J., & Rosenthal, B. (1995). Interdisciplinary and interorganizational collaboration. In A. Minahan, *Encyclopedia of social work, Vol. II* (19th ed., pp. 1479–1489). Silver Springs, MD: National Association of Social Workers.

Adam. (2008, April 7). Car dealers and manufacturers compete for online ad space. Retrieved May 21, 2011, from Blogpro Automotive website: http://blogproautomotive.com/internet-marketing/car-dealers-and-manufacturers-compete-for-online-ad-space/

Ahuja, G. (2000). The duality of collaboration: Inducements and opportunities in the formation of interfirm linkages. *Strategic Management Journal*, 317–343.

Audi, T. (2009, December 30). L.A. gangs seek profit in peace. Retrieved June 4, 2010, from *Wall Street Journal* website: http://online.wsj.com/article/SB126213528444809699.html

Brignull, H. (2009, October 9). Just add an egg—Usability, user experience, and dramaturgy. Retrieved June 1, 2011, from 90 percent of everything website: http://www.90percentofeverything.com/2009/10/20/just-add-an-egg-usability-user-experience-and-dramaturgy/

Business Dictionary. (n.d.). Business resources. Retrieved April 1, 2010, from Business Dictionary: http://www.businessdictionary.com/definition/business-resources.html

Business Dictionary. (n.d.). Cooperation. Retrieved April 1, 2010, from Business Dictionary: http://www.businessdictionary.com/definition/cooperation.html

Business Dictionary. (n.d.). Coordination. Retrieved April 1, 2010, from Business Dictionary: http://www.businessdictionary.com/definition/coordination.html

Byrne, T. (2010, March 31). How to use internal collaboration and social networking technology. Retrieved February 23, 2011, from Inc. website: http://www.inc.com/guides/2010/03/internal-collaboration-and-social-media-technology.html

Center for Innovation. (n.d.). What we do: Design Research Studio. Center for Innovation website: http://centerforinnovation.mayo.edu/sparc.html

Clinovations. (n.d.). Clinovations collaborative. Retrieved May 15, 2011, from Clinovations website: http://www.clinovations.com/clinovations-collaborative.htm

Collins, J. C., & Porras, J. I. (1996, September-October). Building Your Company's Vision. *Harvard Business Review.* Retrieved August 31, 2011, from http://www.thenextstepprogram.com.au/uploads/File/Building%20a%20Vision.pdf

CPA Global. (2010). Industry collaboration: A new era of open innovation. *CPA Global White Papers.*

Dettmer, A. (2011, April 25). Missouri American Water supports national prescription drug. Retrieved May 10, 2011, from American Water website: http://files.shareholder.com/downloads/AMERPR/0x0x461819/c66049cb-c8ee-4ea6-bfa8-ad5afefa7ab9/Take-Back_Day.pdf

Ditkoff, M., Moore, T., Allen, C., & Pollard, D. (2005, November). The ideal collaborative team. Retrieved November 10, 2010, from Idea Champions website: http://www.ideachampions.com/downloads/collaborationresults.pdf

Dosh, K. (2011, April 25). How much does the BCS top 25 spend on recruiting? Retrieved June 8, 2011, from *Forbes* website: http://blogs.forbes.com/sportsmoney/2011/04/25/how-much-does-the-bcs-top-25-spend-on-recruiting/?partner=contextstory

Drucker, P. F. (1989, July 25). Drucker on management: Sell the mailroom. *Wall Street Journal.*

Edgar SEC Filings. (2011, August 9). *Edgar SEC Filings.* Retrieved August 18, 2011, from http://www.sec.gov/Archives/edgar/data/1300514/000095012311074643/c18676e10vq.htm

Eli Lilly and Company. (2011, April 26). Lilly and Medtronic announce drug-device collaboration for Parkinson's disease. Retrieved May 25, 2011, from Eli Lilly website: https://investor.lilly.com/releasedetail2.cfm? ReleaseID=571796

Elkington, J. (1998). *Cannibals with forks: The triple bottom line of 21st century business.* Gabriola Island, BC: New Society Publishers.

Encarta. (2001). *Microsoft Encarta college dictionary.* New York: Bloomsbury Publishing.

Erickson, T. J. (2010, November). Building organizations to leverage collaborative technologies. Retrieved January 5, 2011, from Moxie White Paper: http://www.tammyerickson.com/images/uploads/Building_Organizations_to_Leverage_Collaborative_Technologies_-_White_Paper_11–10.pdf

Erkip, S. S. (n.d.). An analysis of manufacturer benefits under vendor managed systems. Retrieved May 21, 2011, from Bilkent University website: http://www.ie.bilkent.edu.tr/~ie571/Savasaneril%20Erkip2010.pdf

Farmer, W. (2009, April 7). Trust and collaboration. Retrieved February 7, 2011, from Word Gravity website: http://wordgravity.blogspot.com/2009/04/trust-and-collaboration.html

FiercePharma. (2011, April 21). Pfizer and Shanghai Pharmaceutical sign memorandum of understanding for potential strategic partnership. Retrieved August 30, 2011, from http://www.fiercepharma.com/press_releases/pfizer-and-shanghai-pharmaceutical-sign-memorandum-understanding-potential--0

Fritscher, L. (2008, September 15). About.com: Phobias. Retrieved August 30, 2010, from http://phobias.about.com/od/glossary/g/groupthinkdef.htm

Frost & Sullivan. (n.d.). Meetings around the world II: Charting the course of advanced collaboration. A Frost & Sullivan Whitepaper Sponsored by Verizon and Cisco. Retrieved from http://www.verizonbusiness.com/resources/whitepapers/wp_meetings-around-the-world-ii_en_xg.pdf

GE Energy. (n.d.). Customer collaboration. Retrieved June 13, 2011, from GE Energy website: http://site.ge-energy.com/online_tools/collaboration/en/index.htm

Goetz, K. (2011, February 1). How 3M gave everyone days off and created an innovation dynamo. Retrieved June 25, 2011, from Fast Co. Design website: http://www.fastcodesign.com/1663137/how-3m-gave-everyone-days-off-and-created-an-innovation-dynamo

Gray, L. (2009, February 13). Honey bees work together to make group decisions. Retrieved March 3, 2010, from *Telegraph* website: http://www.telegraph.co.uk/earth/wildlife/4601179/Honey-bees-work-together-to-make-group-decisions.html

Griffith, T. (2010, September 9). Nucor steel: Transportation recovery through systems savvy management. Retrieved April 4, 2011, from Technology & Organizations blog: http://www.terrigriffith.com/blog/2010/09/09/nucor-steel-transportation-recovery-systems-savvy-management/

Hackman, J. R. (2011, June 7). Six common misperceptions about teamwork. Retrieved July 1, 2011, from *Harvard Business Review* website: http://blogs.hbr.org/cs/2011/06/six_common_misperceptions_abou.html

HAI Watch. (n.d.). HAI Watch partners. Retrieved January 15, 2011, from HAI Watch website: http://en.haiwatch.com/Partners.aspx

Hansen, M. T. (2009, November 9). Collaboration done right. (P. Shaplen, Interviewer).

Himmelman, A. T. (1993). *ARCH National Resource Center.* Raleigh, NC.

Hollis, J. (2008). *What matters most.* New York: Gotham.

HPC Wire. (2008, February 27). Sun, Chinese government announce OpenSPARC collaboration. Retrieved August 10, 2011, from HPC Wire website: http://archive.hpcwire.com/hpc/2171655.html

Huston, L., & Sakkab, N. (2006). Connect and develop: Inside Procter & Gamble's new model for innovation. *Harvard Business Review*: http://hbr.org/2006/03/connect-and-develop-inside-procter-gambles-new-model-for-innovation/ar/1

Hypercompetition: Financial Times Lexicon. (n.d.). Retrieved July 6, 2010, from http://lexicon.ft.com/term.asp?t=hypercompetition

IBM Global Business Services. (2006). Global CEO study 2006. Retrieved April 8, 2010, from http://www-07.ibm.com/smb/includes/content/industries/electronics/pdf/Global_CEO_Study_-_Electronics.pdf

Indinopulos, M. (2011, June 17). Enterprise Social Software blog. Retrieved June 20, 2011, from Socialtext website: http://www.socialtext.com/blog/

Interlink Management Consulting. (n.d.). Mergers integration. Retrieved January 15, 2011, from Interlink Business website: http://interlinkbusiness.com/mergers.html

Janis, I. L. (1972). *Victims of groupthink.* Boston: Houghton-Mifflin.

Jaroslovsky, R. (2011, May 31). You never knew you wanted these gadgets. *San Francisco Chronicle*, p. A1.

Kanellos, M. (2010, April 22). 10 Green giants that could change the world. *CBS News: The Green Eye.*

Kaufman, M. (2006, December 19). NASA launches Google collaboration. *Washington Post*: http://www.washingtonpost.com/wp-dyn/content/article/2006/12/18/AR2006121801119.html

Landi, H. (2010, August 3). Apple & Eve: Good to the core. Retrieved December 10, 2010, from *Beverage World* website: http://www.beverage world.com/index.php?option=com_content&view=article&id=38445: apple-and-eve-good-to-the-core&catid=105:featured-content

Leadbeater, C. (2005, July). Charles Leadbeater on innovation. Retrieved July 1, 2011, from TED website: http://www.ted.com/talks/charles_leadbeater_on_innovation.html

Lister, K. (2010, September). Making the most of freelance talent. Retrieved December 10, 2010, from *Entrepreneur* website: http://www.entrepreneur.com/article/217195

MacKenzie, K. (2011). Highlights from 2011 Best Places to Work for Recent Grads. Retrieved August 31, 2011, from http://www.experience.com/entry-level-jobs/2011-best-places-to-work/highlights-from-2011-best-places-to-work/

McNabb, A. I., & O'Neill, K. E. (1996). *Small firm, large firm collaboration for survival.* Newtownabbey, Northern Ireland: Ulster Business School.

Mediratta, B., & Bick, J. (2007, October 21). The Google way: Give engineers room. *New York Times.*

Mergen, M. (2004, August 15). Rowing teaches teamwork lessons. Retrieved June 3, 2011, from *USA Today* website: http://www.usatoday.com/money/companies/management/2004–08–15-lyons-advice_x.htm

Merriam-Webster. (n.d.). *Merriam-Webster Online.* Retrieved April 1, 2010, from http://www.merriam-webster.com/dictionary/networking

Microsoft. (2006, June 5). Microsoft News Center. Retrieved June 30, 2011, from Microsoft website: http://www.microsoft.com/presspass/press/2006/jun06/06–05VerizonBusinessCollaborationPR.mspx

Moore, W. (2010). Innovation lessons from Silly Putty. *Innovation Tools*: http://www.innovationtools.com/Articles/ArticleDetails.asp?a=525

NASA. (1986). *Report of the Presidential Commission on the Space Shuttle Challenger Accident.* Retrieved January 26, 2011, from NASA website: http://science.ksc.nasa.gov/shuttle/missions/51-l/docs/rogers-commission/table-of-contents.html

Nelson, A. (2011, January 11). How mapping, SMS platforms saved lives in Haiti earthquake. Retrieved June 17, 2011, from PBS website: http://www.pbs.org/mediashift/2011/01/how-mapping-sms-platforms-saved-lives-in-haiti-earthquake011.html

Nike. (2010, January 27). Organizations call for greater open innovation to advance sustainability. Retrieved March 15, 2010, from Nike Biz website: http://www.nikebiz.com/media/pr/2010/01/27_GreenXchange.html

Northern Illinois University. (2005). Responsible conduct of research. Retrieved January 6, 2011, from Responsible Conduct of Research (RCR) website at Northern Illinois University: http://ori.hhs.gov/education/products/niu_collabresearch/collabresearch/need/need.html

Novogratz, J. (2006, March 1). When was the last time you really looked at a flower? Retrieved January 8, 2011, from Acumen Fund website: http://blog.acumenfund.org/2006/03/01/when-was-the-last-time-you-really-looked-at-a-flower/

Oak Ridge National Laboratory. (2000). Human genome project information. Retrieved April 4, 2011, from Oak Ridge National Laboratory website: http://www.ornl.gov/sci/techresources/Human_Genome/resource/media.shtml

Ohnsman, A. (2010, October 7). Bloomberg. Retrieved October 15, 2010, from Bloomberg website: http://www.bloomberg.com/news/2010-10-07/toyota-displays-tesla-supplied-electric-rav4-to-u-s-dealers-in-las-vegas.html

Paddock, M. (2011, February 1). 2011 guide to grants—New direction from the Preparedness Task Force. Retrieved March 2, 2011, from Homeland Security Today website: http://www.hstoday.us/resources/hstoday-guide-to-grants/single-article/2011-guide-to-grants-new-direction-from-the-preparedness-task-force/0f42303ce9170ff6749792769515d684.html

Papadellis, R. (2010, September 15). Ocean Spray's secrets of co-op success. (R. Reiss, interviewer). http://www.forbes.com/2010/09/15/papadellis-ocean-spray-leadership-managing-interview.html

Policy and Medicine. (2009, October 20). Continuing education to prevent infection: Collaboration to save lives. Retrieved May 25, 2011, from *Policy and Medicine* website: http://www.policymed.com/2009/10/continuing-education-to-prevent-infection-collaboration-to-save-lives.html

Porat, M. U. (1977). *The information economy: Definition and measurement.* Washington, D.C.: Superintendent of Documents, U.S. Government Printing Office.

Print Place Blog. (2009, June 4). How to collaborate with other companies the smart way.

Procter & Gamble. (n.d.). Connect & develop. Retrieved July 10, 2011, from P&G website: https://secure3.verticali.net/pg-connection-portal/ctx/noauth/0_0_1_4_83_4_6.do

Raisch, S., & Birkinshaw, J. (2008, March 14). Organizational ambidexterity: Antecedents, outcomes, and moderators. *Journal of Management.* http://jom.sagepub.com/content/34/3/375.abstract

Retail Touch Points. (2011, April 21). Ahold USA reports time and cost savings via trade promotion collaboration. Retrieved May 21, 2011, from Retail Touch Points website: http://www.retailtouchpoints.com/retail-store-ops/849-ahold-usa-reports-time-and-cost-savings-via-trade-promotion-collaboration.

Roberts, J. (2005, February). Organizing for performance: How BP did it. Retrieved June 25, 2011, from Stanford Graduate School of Business website: http://www.gsb.stanford.edu/news/bmag/sbsm0502/feature_bp.shtml

Robinson, M. (2009, November 20). MUJI x LEGO Collaboration. http://the189.com/style/fashion/muji-x-lego-collaboration/

Ryan, T. (2007, October 22). The slow path to trade promotion collaboration. Retrieved March 7, 2011, from Retail Wire website: http://www.retailwire.com/discussion/12501/the-slow-path-to-trade-promotion-collaboration

Saveri, A. (n.d.). Institute for the Future. Retrieved April 1, 2010, from http://www.iftf.org/system/files/deliverables/SR-851A_New_Literacy_Cooperation.pdf

Schmitz, B. (2011, March 22). Protecting intellectual property. Retrieved April 4, 2011, from Creo website: http://creo.ptc.com/2011/03/22/protecting-intellectual-property/

Sharma, M. (2011, June 8). ID-only shopping encourages Wal-Mart in India where retail is off limits. Retrieved July 15, 2011, from Bloomberg: http://www.bloomberg.com/news/2011–06–08/id-only-shopping-encourages-wal-mart-to-open-stores-in-india.html

Shirky, C. (2008, September 19). Clay Shirky (shirky.com) It's Not Information Overload. It's Filter Failure. New York: Web 2.0 Expo. Retrieved August 30, 2011, from http://blip.tv/web2expo/web-2-0-expo-ny-clay-shirky-shirky-com-it-s-not-information-overload-it-s-filter-failure-1283699

Shiva, V. (1993). *Monocultures of the mind: Biodiversity, biotechnology, and agriculture.* New Delhi: Zed Pressi.

Sinclair, M. (2011, April 25). Collaboration and performance appraisal. Retrieved May 10, 2011, from Melinda Sinclair website: http://melindasinclair.com/collaboration-and-performace-appraisal/

Slater, L. (n.d.). Collaboration: A framework for school improvement. Retrieved May 15, 2011, from *International Electronic Journal for Leadership in Learning* website: http://iejll.synergiesprairies.ca/iejll/index.php/iejll/article/view/698/358

Sloane, P. (2004, March 9). *Innovation Tools.* Retrieved October 15, 2010, from *Innovation Tools* website: http://www.innovationtools.com/Articles/EnterpriseDetails.asp?a=128

Steiner, C. (2009, February 16). The creativity of crowds. *Forbes.*

Surowiecki, J. (2004). *The wisdom of crowds.* New York: Doubleday.

Tanna, B., & Kelley, G. (2011, February 15). Pharmaceutical industry rapidly expanding partnerships with new entrants in health care space. Retrieved May 1, 2011, from Ernst & Young website: http://www.ey.com/Publication/vwLUAssets/News_release_20110215/$FILE/News%20release%20 20110215%20-%20Pharmaceutical%20industry%20rapidly%20expand ing%20partnerships%20with%20new%20entrants%20in%20health%20 care%20space.pdf

The Riley Guide. (n.d.). Networking & your job search. Retrieved April 1, 2010, from http://www.rileyguide.com/network.html

The Sustainability Consortium. (n.d.). About the Consortium. Retrieved May 15, 2011, from Sustainability Consortium website: http://www.sustainabili tyconsortium.org/why-we-formed/

Tuffley, D. (2004). Master of philosophy thesis. Retrieved June 6, 2011, from Griffith University: http://www4.gu.edu.au:8080/adt-root/uploads/ approved/adt-QGU20050822.155303/public/02Main.pdf

Tugwell, P., Welch, V., Ueffing, E., Ortiz, Z., Nasser, M., Waters, E., et al. (2008, October 3). Evaluating the priority setting processes used across the Cochrane Collaboration: Accountability, reasonability, and equity. Retrieved March 17, 2011, from Slideshare website: http://www.slideshare.net/monal isa2n/evaluating-the-priority-setting-processes-used-across-the-cochrane-collaboration

UNESCO. (2006, October 26). Radio station at the National University of Rwanda. Retrieved April 1, 2010, from http://portal.unesco.org/en/ev.php-URL_ID=34387&URL_DO=DO_TOPIC&URL_SECTION=201.html

U.S. Department of State. (2011, May 25). U.S.-China Strategic and Economic Dialogue 2010 Outcomes of the Strategic Track. Retrieved August 10, 2011, from http://www.state.gov/r/pa/prs/ps/2010/05/142180.htm

USA for Africa. (2010, January 28). *We Are The World @ 25.* Retrieved May 25, 2011, from USA for Africa website: http://www.usaforafrica.org/watw25.html

Westley, F., & Vredenburg, H. (1997). Interorganizational collaboration and the preservation of global biodiversity. *Organization Science,* 381–403.

Zuckerman, E. (2011, January 14). The first Twitter revolution? Retrieved June 16, 2011, from *Foreign Policy* website: http://www.foreignpolicy.com/articles/ 2011/01/14/the_first_twitter_revolution?page=0,1

ABOUT THE AUTHOR

Dan Sanker is the founder, CEO, and president of CaseStack, a company that has been recognized as one of the fastest-growing companies in the United States by *Inc.*, *Entrepreneur*, and PricewaterhouseCoopers. Under his leadership, the company has been chosen as "One of the Best Places to Work," and noted for its innovative technology and collaborative relationships. Sanker has held leadership positions at Procter & Gamble, Nabisco, Deloitte, and KPMG.

He has been published, quoted, or profiled in numerous publications including the *Washington Post* and the *Los Angeles Times*. He has been named a finalist for Ernst & Young Entrepreneur of the Year Awards multiple times. He received his MBA from the Anderson Graduate School of Management at UCLA and attended Kansai University in Japan, University of London, and Institute for European Studies in Austria. Sanker was recognized as a "Green Supply Chain Professional to Know," and he was a founder of the Green Valley Initiative, a collaborative economic development organization promoting sustainability technology.

INDEX